FACTS, LIES, AND QUALITY MANAGEMENT

Suresh Kumar Krishnan

PARTRIDGE
A Penguin Random House Company

To order additional copies of this book, contact
Toll Free 800 101 2657 (Singapore)
Toll Free 1 800 81 7340 (Malaysia)
orders.singapore@partridgepublishing.com

www.partridgepublishing.com/singapore

ACKNOWLEDGEMENT

I would like to thank my parents, wife and children, siblings, relatives, teachers and my dearest friends for all the support and encouragements....Stay Beautiful as you always are.

CONTENTS

PART 1

The Awareness:
Quality and Quality Thinking

The one word, which we fall back to when describing satisfaction or delight after having consumed a product or service, is the buzz word 'Quality'. The use of the word 'Quality' can be seen and heard everywhere regardless of the types of product or services being promoted or talked about. However there's still a very vague understanding of this universally used word in many aspects. Of course, if you have asked ten different people on what is quality to them relating to a particular product or service, you will definitely hear ten different answers. This is because different people may have different expectations and needs depending on the situation they are in. So, we can certainly say that *quality to an individual is something that gave him/her a degree of satisfaction and delight through a holistic experience that created value to them*.

On the other hand, it is quite common for people to label Quality of product or service using the term 'Low Quality' and 'High Quality'. For instance, when asked, between BMW car and a locally made car such as Kancil (Malaysia), which is higher in quality? It is no surprise if we hear that BMW is higher quality than a locally made car. If we accept this answer as true, than we are claiming that there are organizations out there which produce low quality products and furthermore say that there are people in the society who go for low quality products or services. The main reason why we hear such things is solely because of the failure to understand a product or service's specification and the type of value created. Here people should know that the specification and value (based on one's needs) of a product or service would determine its price. The difference in the pricing of a product or service is determined by the attributes that measure the quality. In the case of a car, the attributes that measure quality can be engine performance, comfort and space, after sales service, safety features, design and aesthetics, reliability and even the consumption. This means the Kancil has its quality and the BMW has its quality based on an individual's needs. By the way, you don't want to be driving a BMW to the nearest train station from your house every day to commute further right.

So, what should be understood here is also that, while the attributes to measure quality when purchasing a car can be the same for any brand, the capacity of each attribute mentioned (could even be more) will determine the price. Different attributes to measure quality will be present for every product or service, example when you want to measure the quality of food, the attributes to look for should be the portion, texture, temperature, display, nutritional value, aroma, taste and so on. If we don't get the value for the money paid for the food due the lacking in any of the attributes, it will lead to a bad experience. However, do take note that price of food is also determined by where are you having it, the place (ambiance) does matter. Again, to measure the quality of the ambiance there will other related attributes to look into. This is the reason why, many feedback forms out there don't measure the right things and left for customers to fill for the sake of having them.

It is very clear here that a highly priced product or service need not necessarily mean that it would satisfy, delight or create value for anyone all the time. It all depends on the holistic experiences created by the product or service at that point in time or every other time using them. The cheapest of product or service can be appreciated and seen as very high quality, as long it can perform the way it was expected to and create the rightful holistic experience for an individual or group.

So, today we cannot say that Quality is very abstract or very difficult to measure and so on. If we can understand what will satisfy, delight or create value, then, that will be the attributes to measure the quality of a product or service. The capacity (what can be seen or presented) of a particular attribute is later quantified to determine the price of a particular product or service. As long that there's value for the money paid by a customer for a product or service, then he or she will feel that Quality was experienced.

The Qualities of Quality – The three phases

Any product or service must go through three phases of outputs where quality will and must be in control in order to create the right outcome(s) or the Quality in total realization. The phases are described as below:

- **Q1**: Quality in terms of specifications of design inputs (include verification and validation), process controls (quality check points) and product or service output. Here activities such as inspections, testing and monitoring can be applied using various tools and techniques to ensure that the final product or service meets the requirements. At this point the realization of the product or service happens and may include the packaging as well for delivery. Quality checks will be performed in order to ensure the product or service met its intended requirements.

- **Q2**: Quality of a product or service at this point can be seen in terms of presentation, more added packaging, marketing, branding, transportation, storage and distribution. Here the product or services is attached with the right aesthetics that should create customer and end user delight to purchase. This can happen from the point of product or service realization (Q1) or totally at a new location which suits best. At this point, creation of visualization of experiences that relates to individuals needs can also be seen. This includes examples such as test driving a brand new car model or any vehicles, watch video of amazing holidays, free sample given for testing new product or services, free seminars, free food testing and so on.

- **Q3**: Quality is seen from the perspective of the ability of a particular product or service to create the right experiences for the customer or end user as portrayed in Q1 and Q2, which leads them to finally say they have got a Quality product or service. This is the part where the customer or the end user's experiences have touched their belief system (positively or negatively). Only then we will realize the totality of Quality, where by the customer or end user will come back for more. This also means that value creation has also happened. The ultimate feedback regarding a product or service that will alter the course of phase 1 and phase 2 in the future happens here.

Based on the 3 phases of quality described above, we must take note that all the 3 phases mentioned can happen at one point and with all happening at one time or multiple points and happening at various point in time. Also be clear that the path way to realizing totality in Quality of a particular product or service can happen directly from Q1 to Q3 for certain product or service (direct from the production to end user) or goes through all the phases that is from Q1 to Q2 and Q2 to Q3. However as mentioned above, the experiences from Q3 will determine whether Q1 and Q2 will ever happen again or change (invention, innovation or improvement) will be required for a particular product or service. The overwhelming build-up given (Q1 and Q2) for a particular product or service can help in the sales. However, whether there will be continuous repeated sales will certainly depend on the Q3 phase.

Whatever the case, this is how quality must be seen and not in a mutually exclusive circumstance for a particular product or service. So, what should be understood and realized here is that *Quality of a product or service does not end with specifications but more about the ability of these specifications transforming into experiences that rock the belief system of an individual customer or end user.* Failure to understand this, will lead to a very early demise of a particular product or service regardless of types of industries or businesses out there. At this point, *Quality can be defined as* below:

"Quality is achieved when the experiences rocks the Belief System of an Individual and not just by attaining the specifications of its attributes"

Many efforts took place throughout the world by countries, societies, organizations or even individuals in making sure that whatever produced, tangible or intangible (products and services) has its level of required Qualities. Different products will have its unique set of attributes that will measure the Quality. Well, with that in mind, Quality thinking certainly has evolved over time from Quality Inspection (QI) to Quality Control (QC) then to Quality Assurance (QA), from QA to Quality Management System (QMS) and of course with the hope one day of having Total Quality Management (TQM) or Manage Quality in Total (MQT) or even Quality of Management in Total (QMT). Whichever way we want it or call it, one should realize that while we are moving, the dynamism of Quality is inevitable. While it took longer time those days but the implementation phase of any new ideas has certainly become more rapid with time. These inevitable movements must be understood as the evolution of the human mind which in return makes things that was slow before to be done much faster today. Having said this, we should view Quality beyond the specifications that measure it. Time has come, where we must stop being satisfied with producing products or services that merely meets the specifications of output but go further into outcomes that create the right experiences for the end user.

In life we tend to spend our money on a lot of things, which could be tangible or even intangible. Whatever the product or services, we should realize is that our purchase goes beyond the attributes (specifications) of the product or service. Quality product or service must be measured by looking into the holistic experiences gained from the usage of a particular product and not just at the point of monetary transactions. Let's look at the scenario below:

"I went to eat at a famous fish head curry restaurant, the curry is so tasty that they even produce and sell their own curry paste. On that day, I ordered as usual for two person and we were there between 1.30pm -2.00pm which is pretty much still the lunch hour. The thing

that I asked was for papadam (spicy Indian crackers) that should be easily available and also quickly made. However, while the fish head curry meal was good but the answer given by the waiter that the papadam is finished is unacceptable. This was further disturbed us when a group of enforcement officers who came at the next table were provided with the papadam when they requested. So, our experience was not pleasant after that. At this point, while we are satisfied with the specification of the product but the holistic experience gained has certainly touched our earlier belief system. We now believe there's no value for the money we spent at that restaurant. Quality is bad, lesson learned"

As mentioned earlier, existence of the 3 phases of quality where a product or services go through can certainly be seen in the situation above. It's all about the holistic experiences realized by an individual or group, which in turn ends by the creation of value for the customer or the end user. Achieving specification of a given product or service can be easily done but creating the right experiences that brings a person to the next level, can be a big challenge. Again, there must be some effort in doing so at all times at every level, only then we can satisfy, delight or create value for any interested parties in this era.

Jump on to the bandwagon – everyone is doing it

Quality must exist in whatever that we are doing or planning (thinking) to do at all times. Quality must be built into the product or service that we are producing, which also means that quality should also be built into an organization (regardless of business types) and how actually we want to do that? This is the biggest challenge to most organizations that are craving for various desired achievements, excellence and quality. In order to achieve such an outcome there should be many sustainable quality improvement programs and activities in place. So, many organizations embark into various quality initiatives as this has become somewhat like a fashion to do it in recent times. Of course this also leads to the creation of many indicators or performance measures that will be used to monitor whether or not a particular process and all the activities within that process is in control. These measures were also used as measure of departmental and individual performance. As such, it became important to make sure we achieve those set targets without worrying about how we got there.

However it must realized that indicators or performance measures could only give information to a certain extent. This is because in most cases the underlying errors in various types of activities are not eliminated yet. These indicators or performance measures will certainly give us some information on the efficiency level of a process or the activities within the process. *Unfortunately, we may never know whether we are doing all the right things or wrong things very correctly.* In order to avoid such situations we must look into the ideas of eliminating all types of failure events or potential failures within an organization. One way to really know your organization is by understanding the existence of all types of failure events and the potential failures that may take place. This means the quality improvement programs in place at an organization must include the ideas of accepting that failure events and potential failures exist, identifying them and finally reducing or eliminating them totally from the organizational system. This is certainly in line with the current emphasis on risk management.

Quality Thinking isn't about checking Quality at the end of a production assembly line, it's beyond all that. Quality Thinking must be there at any place and all the time. The thing about knowledge attained during courses or workshops related to Quality Management are seen as something that should only be used at their work place. However, it's a fact that people draw the line between the work they do to earn a living and the other part of their daily life. The thoughts and thinking about Quality is demonstrated only during work hours (at times, it also requires the right enforcements). Absents of such noble thoughts can be noticed here and there, almost everywhere day to day of our life.

Let me share a scenario that happens all the time when people go to places of worship regardless of what religion, we tend find situations where places are jammed with vehicles that block the roads due to double or triple parking. This leads traffic congestions that disrupt other people's livelihood. Imagine if there was an ambulance that needs to go to the hospital urgently or to a scene of an accident, what have these people who are praying have done? There's no single religion in the world that tells anyone that you must pray, even if you have to create inconvenience for others. What we see out there is simply the lack of Quality Thinking. The situation tells us one thing for sure **"Creating chaos outside the place of worship, in order to seek the peace inside".**

In this modern time we are able to utilize a lot of sophisticated inventions that ease the human life in many ways. However, with such technology, the impact it creates in our surrounding must be controlled as well. So, the mind must evolve with these rapid changes in order to continue creating the right experiences in our short lifetime. In life we go through all kind of experiences which may be good, bad or even ugly. Whatever the experiences it may be, it will teach us some kind of lesson which will increase our knowledge in certain matters and further strengthens our Beliefs in a particular issue. These Beliefs will eventually set the mode of our attitude and behaviour in any kind of situation that we may face in our life time.

Telecommunication and its technological abilities today can be said as one of the greatest invention and also the most *influential invasion* into an individual's day to day life. The smartphones that all walks of life carry today can create all kinds of negative experiences to its users and the people around them. This is again a topic of *being in control* of the situation or *being controlled by* the situation where a smart phone is being used. We can't deny anymore that this technology has certainly affected our Quality of Life and the people around us with numerous types of experiences. Once again the experiences could have created positive manifestation of attitude and behaviour or otherwise negatively. However, whatever the experiences are, it will certainly touch the Belief system of an individual with whatever deemed right or wrong for a particular situation.

"A lot of people have been driving a car to reach their desired destination for a very-very long time, as far as the early 1900. However, with the increase in technological enhancement in the automotive industry, we can definitely say that we are experiencing better mobility from one location to another with greater comfort and ease. While this matter continuously happens in one side, the invasions of the telecommunication devices have certainly influenced the way we handle those automobiles today. Every day we hear of accidents caused by people who are so hooked to their smartphones and other gadgets, due to loss of concentration on the road. Again, the absence of Quality thinking in many ways can cause various problems that may even lead to death. It must also be made known to everyone that the phone can be smart but certainly not the user, unless we take relevant precautionary measures at all times."

What can be seen here again is that, control must be present beyond the production assembly line of a particular product or service. It's kind of similar to ensuring the disposal of an item after use, for example the way to dispose chewing gum. There are clear descriptions on how to dispose the chewing gum so that it doesn't create problems for the environment and people. *So, phase3 of Quality isn't just about the product or service delivered but also its impact to the non-users as well.* These components of experiences from phase Q1 to Q3 of Quality must be for seen from the beginning as much as possible. Here, the risks involved and the level of risk appetite of a particular product or service would create must be known and it's deemed to be dynamic in nature. *Risk appetite can be defined as 'the amount and type of risk that an organisation is willing to take (that gives the tolerances) in order to meet their strategic objectives and outcomes.*

"Quality Reasons" for not looking into weaknesses

The most usual reason that I hear on why certain tasks never get done is lack of staff or manpower. This reason is quite common in most organizations, especially in the government sector. Due to this, should we only do what we can and forget the rest of it?

Let's look into a scenario, a government agency staff has to conduct a number of programs every year (within an allocated budget) in his district on Quit Smoking Campaign. Over time these types of programs should reduce the number of smokers among the youth, that is of course one of the many outcomes (the kinds of experiences created to touch their belief system) that would be expected. However when you question the staff on whether we have achieved those outcome(s), the reason that was given is that to quantify such things we don't have enough manpower. Of course followed by another reason that, it was what we've been doing all these years and accepted as a norm (the legacy syndrome).

This is where one must "think outside the box" (again which box?, we shall discuss this in detail later); in such lacking we should be able to create a system that make us achieve what we suppose to and not give "Quality reasons" for not doing so. If your service provider, for example water supply service were to tell you that there will be cuts in your area for the next 5 days, what would be your actions towards the variation in the current system? Are you going stop taking bath for the next 5 days? Are you going reduce water intake in your cooking? Are you going stop cleaning at home? Most likely the answer to all those questions would be "NO", what you would have done is, create a system within the weakness (which is certainly beyond your control) by storing water with whatever means in order to reduce the variation of how things have been before the water cut. This would certainly give the right experiences to deal with problems even with limitations."*Quality thinking" will always take us through, NOT "Quality Reasons"*

Forgive, Forget and Move on
(Could be easier said than done)

It's certainly is an undeniable fact that the thought of forgiving for ones mistakes directly or indirectly would be a sensible thing to do. Yes the concept and benefits of Forgiveness have been explored in religious thoughts, social science and also medicine. Holding grudges or taking revenge may not help in the long run for whichever party for that matter and the impact can be from various aspects for sure. I bet that you have heard the phrase "Forgive, forget & move on" at least once by now. Well, I think we better take another look at this phrase; this is because a major flaw can be contributed by the word "forget".

The problem with people is that they forget just too quickly, no matter the incident involves them directly, indirectly or not at all.

When a failure event happens one should be learning on what when wrong and certainly should ensure it doesn't repeat again. The reason for many repeated failure events in our life time is just simply because people fail to realize it's just not about forgiving, forgetting and moving on. Every individual is here for a reason, it could be a long stay or a short one it doesn't matter but what is their respective contribution to mankind as a whole is what matters (could be good, bad or even ugly). The important thing to note here is that, **"Making mistakes is a norm but NOT learning from it should never be our culture"**. Again, we have also heard that it's alright to make mistakes because we can learn from the mistake (experiences, knowledge and exposures to rock the current belief system) that we made, very true indeed but one should also realize that we can't make all the mistakes ourselves. We should also be learning from other people's mistakes as well. This brings us to the point to note that is, we at times are unable to link ourselves with another individual's experience with a particular failure event. That's why we feel it's fine to make the mistakes on our own.

It's certainly undeniable that challenges are plenty out there, some catch you knowingly and some unknowingly. When we say caught knowingly such as weather whereby we are able to know that there will be strong typhoon with certain speed going to hit a particular place. We may have the time to prepare and move out or prepared enough to face it. However, even after years of such occurrences people still fail to learn from it and at every occurrence of the same events they just take it as if it was the first time. Till today, we still find same comments from some leadership that we have to review our disaster management standard operating procedures (SOPs) every time after an incident and not before it happened.

Why do we take so long to learn? Why do we forget so quickly? Why unrelated incidents never trigger internal review of systems?

These are some of the questions that everyone should be aware of and somehow must find a way to stop doing the same. While 2014 was filled with various disastrous events around the globe, but one event that will always be remembered is the disappearance of MH370 which will be a great aviation mystery. The disappearance of MH370 a routine flight from Kuala Lumpur, Malaysia to Beijing, China, the downing of MH17 a flight from Amsterdam, Holland to Kuala Lumpur, Malaysia in Ukraine and few other incidents have caught the aviation industry by a big surprise. One last incident of the year 2014 was the disappearance of the Airasia flight QZ8501, which was eventually found after couple of days and why till today we still have emergency beacons from ill-fated aircrafts such as this that cannot be received by other aircrafts, boats and even the satellites? These are some of the many questions that need answers which then will provide a more robust solution for the problems at hand. It will be very disappointing if we never learn quickly enough to avoid such incidents again.

So, moving on by forgetting can be consoling or helpful to those who are directly involved in a bad ordeal but it does not mean that everyone else should forget or the most important thing that is not learning from it in order to move on. Perhaps one must also understand that many things that happen are in a way predictable under controlled condition. The change would only be on the people, place, time and the magnitude of a particular event. If we could see ourselves and relate to those similarities and understand the potential failure events, it could contribute a lot to mankind. *In fact we should also not forget that evolution makes us adapt and understand those gaps much faster than we think in current time.*

PART 2

More Awareness:
Experiences through Variations

Creating the Right Experiences

So, since we talked a lot about experiences, beliefs, attitudes and behaviours, it will be good to know how to create such experiences that will impact an individual positively. A very important knowledge that must be attained before we even think about creating experiences is about the science of Variation. The topic of variation is taught in all statistics related courses. However, this knowledge of variation was further extended in Quality management, whereby variation was used as an indicator to ensure consistency of output. Statistical Thinking a topic where we will discuss on the understanding, measuring, controlling and eliminating all kinds of variations in order to ensure Quality output or outcomes. It was pretty much a topic known by many working in the field of mass production initially but later found its way into the service based industries as well. This was possible after the introduction of **six sigma** program by Motorola. The Motorola Six Sigma model was developed in 1986 when employee Bill Smith proposed a concept aimed at minimizing variability in manufacturing through the standardization of product defect measurement. In 2008, the concept integrated the lean manufacturing methodology of optimizing customer value and reducing waste.

By the way, let's first understand variation in the simplest way relating to our day to day life. Have you had a situation of the feet hurting when using a new pair of shoes? The first wear blisters can be very painful and irritating. While there can be numerous remedies for the occurrences but the understanding of the root cause will avoid any superstitious remedy. The reason for the first wear blisters is simply because of variation. *There's no one size fits all situation out there.* The underlying variations of a situation and circumstances must be always understood before thinking about any approach to addressing the matter. The fact is that when the human body if divided into two, that is between the left and right, we are able to see variation exist at all times. This also the reason for rich football players have their football boots tailor made or customised for each leg.

It should be understood also that variation always exist and the there are no two things in the world exactly the same. The reason why it looks the same from the naked eye is because variation is under control. The challenge to control variation begins way before the birth itself because of the DNA (Deoxyribonucleic acid or DNA is a molecule that contains the instructions an organism needs to develop, live and reproduce). These instructions are found inside every cell, and are passed down from parents to their children). This DNA is the reason for the uniqueness of every individual and variation. We may resemble our parents, but we are never exactly like them. This is because each child gets only some of the DNA each parent carries. About half our DNA comes from our mother, and half comes from our father. Which pieces we get is basically random, and each child gets a different subset of the parents' DNA.

Thus, siblings may have the same parents, but they usually do not have exactly the same DNA.

So, if any parent use the same approaches to handle their children (each one of them), then they are sure enough to face some trouble. As mentioned above, while a child may resemble the parents but it must be accepted that they are a different individual. They may need different guidance and attention as compared to another child, regardless of the child being male or female. The basic understanding of variation will certainly give us the upper hand to handle all kinds of situation. We are filled with all kinds of variations from the time we wake up in the morning to the time we are back to bed. It's all about the need to understand, quantify, reduce or eliminate all kind of variations in order to have some level of control of the situation.

The same thing happens at a fast food restaurant too. You may have noticed that the people working at a fast food restaurant apart from the permanent staffs are school leavers or students on a semester break came to earn some extra pocket money. This means the turnover of staffs would be high and every time a new hire come in, he or she must learn quickly and start serving. So, how do these types of restaurants keep up having the consistency of their product output? Yes, again the only way to do it is by controlling the variation of each process by having proper policies, procedures, work instructions and also kitchen equipment that performs the same everywhere. If we are able to do this, then there will greater chances of ensuring consistency in output and quality.

Every system has variation; some of this is due to the system itself, known as common cause variation; some of it is due to singular incidents or special situations; this is special cause variation. In his book, *Out of the Crisis* (Massachusetts Institute of Technology,

1982), W. Edwards Deming estimated that 94 percent of problems (or possibilities for improvement) lie with the system as common-cause variation; 6 percent are special causes. The famous Quality Guru, **William Edwards Deming** (October 14, 1900–December 20, 1993) was an American engineer, statistician, professor, author, lecturer, and management consultant.

When we have managed to control the variations within a system or the processes relating to it, we are able to capture various patterns of behaviour. These data will be very helpful in making predictions within the given limit. If outputs and outcomes from systems can be predicted, which means they can be anticipated and managed. We are exposed to all kinds of variations every day and all the time. It's actually up to us to capture these variations that pop up, and decide whether we are to reduce, eliminate or just have it under control. The many examples of variations:

- Traffic flow from your house to any destination from Monday to Sunday for different time, route, weather and season.
- Menu of the daily meals at a day care centre for children, adults, the sick and so on.
- Children at home, each one of them must be seen as an individual. Our love for them can be the same but approaches to handle them will certainly differ.
- The types of customers that visit a service counter at the banks, hospitals, government agencies etc.
- The types of customers at a car park, who might use the parking bay for short or long time and on a particular day longer than the rest.
- The lists can go on and on.

When we are able to capture these types of variations only then we are able to have the right approaches to handle the matter. This is because we are able to see the patterns of behaviour of the system in place, its processes, the people involved, the equipment used, the required environment and also the resources needed. So, if any problems arise, we are able have the right approaches to handle them and bring the variations under control. If variations are not identified and put in controlled condition, then any effort of standardizing a process will be a failure.

Variations to create experiences

As for now, the understanding of variations is that we have to identify, measure, reduce, eliminate or control them. This is how it has always been through the teachings of Statistical Thinking. However, it's time to further explore the contributions of the knowledge regarding variation. The variations must be classified into two different categories:

- Firstly the variations that must be eliminated, reduced or put in controlled condition. This variation is labelled *as Unproductive Variation (UV)*.
- Secondly, the variations that should be created to ensure the first part happen (to eliminate, reduce or put under controlled condition). This variation is labelled *as Productive Variation (PV)*.

Take this scenario as an example:

We are quite used to counter service provision by various organizations out there such as hospitals, banks, local authorities, car service centres and many more. You may have seen that the counters provided by these organizations have been classified to handle different type of needs or types of customers at any one time. Why such classification existed? Yes, because they somehow understood some level of variation that existed within their set of customers. This allowed them to **create variation** in terms of services provided at the respective counter identified to serve them better. So, the simple steps are by categorising the types of customers and their needs. After which different tasks are assigned to the respective staff to handle those different types' customers and their differing needs. In this way we have **created Productive Variations (PVs) to eliminate, reduce or control the Unproductive Variations (UVs)**. Again, this is not the end, the created PV will also have UV that needs to be eliminated, reduced or controlled.

Let's further understand this, a few counters were established at a pharmacy at a government hospital. There were counters to take numbers (normal and for senior citizens) and counters to dispense medicine (for senior citizen and people with disability, for chronic illness and the normal dispense). Clear PV has been created after understanding the types and needs of their customers, well and good. However, the UVs may still pop up in many different situations such as

- *When queue is too long and waiting time too long*
- *The queue number machine not functioning*
- *Error in prescriptions*
- *Doctor's hand writing on the prescription cannot be read*
- *Medicine out of stock*
- *Staff at the counter not competent especially those handling chronic illness*
- *Absenteeism*
- *Language barriers*

What can be understood here is that, we don't always think about eliminating variation all the time but also realize that variation should also be created to solve a problem. After having thought about the right variation in place, also think about the probable UVs that may pop up due to this new solution. These UVs will allow us to understand and quantify the potential risks involved with the new solution and have the organization's risk appetite under control as well.

The steps to create the right experiences are:

1. Understand the needs of a particular situation and the outcomes a solution would provide.
2. Identify the variation that is needed to solve the current condition, Productive Variations (PVs). A better, faster, cheaper or environmentally friendly ways are always encouraged through innovation.
3. Identify the Unproductive Variations (UVs) that may pop up for each of the PVs that have been listed.
4. Eliminate, reduce or control the Unproductive Variations (UVs) between and within the classified PVs. Only then move forward to standardize through a proper set of procedures and works instructions. The steps above will certainly give an organization a better picture about right approaches needed in order to create a holistic experience to enhance Quality of a product.

Once again, the emphasis is so much on creating the right experiences because, when a solution emerges, it should have a very positive impact on the belief system of an individual or group. This will further bring about the desired attitude or behaviour from the experiences to continue using the solution productively. Otherwise any solution to a problem will come to a premature end.

When we are able to gauge and see the level of Productive Variations (PVs) and Unproductive Variations (UVs), only then we will be able to create the holistic experiences needed to achieve Quality. In whatever business out there whether profitable or non-profitable, they are exposed to all kind of variations. *If all these variations (both PVs and UVs) are not identified, people will be doing all the wrong things very correctly and later blame the procedures and work instructions that build in the systems.*

PART 3

The Realization: Quality through Experience Based Outcome (EBO)

Input → Process → Output → Outcome(s)

It's certainly undeniable that achieving an output is pretty much easy as long we stick to the steps that has been written within a procedure. However, the bigger challenge is that when we never take the probable outcomes to an output into consideration from the beginning. We must understand that for every output there could be one or more outcomes. If we never take that into account then we may have written something without foresight in the procedure. This will certainly lead to a mind-set of output based outcome but for quality thinking to prevail me must always look at Outcome based Output.

When people start thinking as far as outcomes in whatever they indulge in, only then we are able to have a clearer view of the destination (what are to be achieved?).

Why do we need Improvement? There is a very simple reason to it, it's because Quality is a Dynamic Phenomenon. Quality Thinking must be seen in everything that anyone does. There must be clear efforts to reduce or eliminate all kinds of failure events that happen around us. *We can't be wasting our limited resources by doing all the wrong things right or the right things wrong.* When we are able to build Quality into whatever that's being done, only then a Quality Outcome can be realized. Let me remind you that, it's rather easy to attain a desired Output but the focus should be further into creating the desired Outcome. So, what we need in people is Outcome based Output mind-sets at all times.

In order to ensure that we have outcome based output, Experience Based Outcome (EBO) is what we should focus on. This is because everything we do in our daily life whether for the first time or numerous times again all depends on the past and present experiences that we have gained. Which means, for us to do something again and again, a particular experience, has touched our Belief System in some way. *So, Quality should not be just defined by meeting specifications or reducing variations, but further into creating experiences that changes the Belief System to say that some level Quality certainly exist.* This means, we should not be always thinking about reducing variation, but rather understand where variation is needed to create the right experiences for Quality. After having achieved this, these variations must be kept under Sustainable Controlled Condition (SCC), where the dynamism is known and captured at all times.

Looking at the notion "Prevention is better than detection" and "Build Quality into the Product", well it's easier said than done. While we have numerous workshops creating various manuals, procedures or work instruction to have a process under control, we still tend to fail in building Quality into the process. What does it actually mean to build Quality into a process? One should realize that creating such documents is not a problem but getting people to use it is what matters. At this point, we must look at the experience gained by the user of the document and also the recipients of the product or service. If the experiences are positive it will touch their Belief System in a positive manner or otherwise. So, building Quality also includes developing the right experiences for the interested parties of a system which is embedded in way we do things. When this happens, doing something correct based on a procedure can become a norm and these positively contributing norms over time will become the quality culture.

There have been numerous occasions where, people are blamed for their attitude and behaviour. It should be realized that attitude and behaviour is merely the manifestations of an individual's Belief system. This Belief system could have been formed through their personal knowledge gained, exposure and experiences. So, expecting people to change their attitude and behaviour without realizing the type of experiences that must be created to have an impact on their Belief system will be a waste of time. This is the same reason for talking about creating the right experiences in any quality initiatives, so that sustainability can also be ensured. When people are exposed to the experiences that had created value for them, they will continue to do the right things. Let's look at the diagram below:

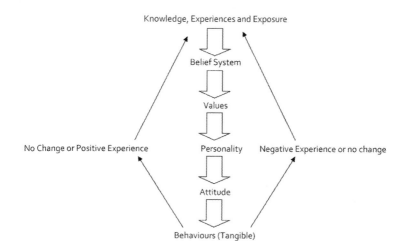

Based on the diagram above, we can see that anything above the behaviours and attitudes cannot be known unless you know the individual personally; even then it's only to a certain extent. However, we still have people talking about attitude and behaviour of an individual as the main problem whenever things go wrong. I believe that the statement like "We have a very good system but the attitude and behaviour of the people here is what makes things go wrong". We must try to what caused all this, because there are a lot of other things that have contributed to the manifestation of such an attitude and behaviour. We must always question on, why people behaved the way that they did? What influenced their behaviours?

If we can take a step back and study the situation, we would be able to understand it takes more than just the attitude to form those unwanted behaviours. We must realize that people have such manifestations of attitudes towards an issue because of the knowledge they have, experiences and exposures they have gained when handling similar situations before. It could have strengthened their beliefs on that particular issue either positively or negatively. This should further enhance the understanding of the definition for Quality, that it's not merely the specifications of attributes belonging to particular product or service. The holistic experiences gained from phase Q1 to Q3 of Quality transformation will rock the Belief system of any individual or group. So, if we are to achieve Total Quality we should be focus on understanding what Beliefs that have formed the current culture. By having a clear understanding on this, we should be able to create the right Productive Variations (PVs) as solutions. These new PVs should provide the suitable experiences and exposures to break the old unwanted culture. Only then all other factors will change its course, like the values, personality and attitude as well as the desired behaviour.

Sustainable Controlled Condition:
With Outcome in Mind

Whenever we plan something, we should try our best to have the end in mind. What kinds of outcome(s) are possible positively or negatively? One example that would give us an idea on this is when we plan our departure to work from home. Of course the first thing is that we must understand the type of variations that exist on the road in all seven days of the week, this would give us idea on when to move out of the house, which route take or avoid and so on. This would include quite a number of factors such as weather, public holidays, school holidays, road closure for certain events, accidents and so on. In the present time there are also technological gadgets to feed real time road traffic information for us to have variations under control. What are we trying to do here? Yes, we are trying to create a controlled condition so that our objectives or intention can be achieved and of course here to reach a particular destination by road on time.

Talking about controlled condition, one should realize to create a good output or best outcomes in whatever that we do, we should look into a sustainable controlled condition, where all Unproductive Variations (UVs) are under control, reduced or eliminated. Again when we say sustainable, it should be realized that we can only create sustainability when we totally understand the dynamism of the system within. This is because Quality is dynamic phenomena. If we fail to understand these matters whatever that we strive to do would fail easily and bound for more repeated failures.

Let's also talk about an accident that happened, where 3 young girls died after falling into the river when the bridge they were crossing gave way. Well, one thing for sure various parties will step in, to find out what happened and of course we will get to the bottom of the matter. Again, what allowed this failure event in the first place? Yes, variations was not understood by the builder (which certainly includes all the relevant parties involved), the building processes before, during and after were certainly not in a controlled condition. Using the same methods, techniques and specifications without realizing the slightest variations that exist will bring about all kinds of problems. Here, the death of three primary school girls, who would have been here if not for the sub-standard bridge. That is the highest price we can pay when we ignore Quality. At this point we also hope that all other bridges being build and all the existing bridges will be kept under sustainable controlled condition, learning from this mistake that happened. Prevention in a pro-active manner will always take us further in many ways.

Quality cases 1 – 'Customers are just stupid, we know better'

Undoubtedly, this is what some service providers think, sadly even at this point in time. There was once I made a complaint to the customer service of a Bank that my request for a top up of existing loan amount after 2 years of repayment. While I was a good pay master, I'm not going to talk about the failure of obtaining the top up loan but what's more disturbing here is that the way the bank managed the whole issue. After making the first complaint, I had about 4 calls from the bank and it's from 4 different people asking me what when wrong. So, repeating the same thing again and again did make me really upset and angry. I know this is not the type of experience that a good customer must go through.

What was very clear here is that, the bank was unable to channel the complaint received in an effective manner and furthermore they don't have a shared database between branches. This is certainly kind of ridiculous in this time where the technology is able to do **wonders** that we never think of. However, when it comes collecting the money from the customers, the banks are able to do **wonders** effectively charging the amount every time a service deemed to have been rendered. So, we **wonder** when this people will ever learn that customers are knowledgeable too.

In another situation, I was paying without any lapses for my car's hire purchase loan for almost 5 years. When it came to the time to sell the existing car and take up a new loan, it was this bank that rejected first on the loan application. It was really an unforeseen situation as a good customer, I had a very high confidence that loan will be approved by the existing bank but it was the first bank to reject my car loan. I was totally upset with this experience. Later I was approached by a bank which I had no previous relationship and was offered a loan from there without much hassle. So, I agreed and immediately removed all accounts from the previous bank. A few days later an employee from the first bank called up from a different branch to convince me that, the loan can still be processed but I refused to entertain.

At this point, what I'm trying to say is that the financial institution like banks should classify the customers (understand variations) even better with the type of information that is available to them. All this should be part of their risk management assessment when it comes to customer related matters. Working in isolation regardless of being under the same umbrella is just to make things worse for the organization as the customers see them as one. Unfortunately, a short sighted organization which looks for immediate profit will never be able to create holistic experiences for their customers which will ensure the Quality of service.

Quality service isn't about providing relevant technologies but at the same time making sure that human touch is always there regardless of the nature of business. Failure to understand such variations will certainly bring about customer dissatisfaction.

Quality cases 2 – Hidden Roles and Responsibility for the society

Entertainment is part of our life. It's undeniable that people seek pleasure through entertainment especially through the music industry. Yes, we do seek such pleasures as it becomes an outlet to release much of our daily tensions of the routines of life. However, as service providers in this area, many fail to provide the best for their customers who spent their money expecting in return to experience a moment of pleasure in that short period of time, probably after work or the weekend night outs.

I walked into many entertainment outlets throughout many countries, however I find it rare to have come across an outlet that takes into account other related factors when it comes to good customer experience apart from dollars and cents. I find that many service providers in the entertainment business are not very holistic in creating experiences for their customers or they are just there for a hit and run business. The few such examples that can be easily related by many, is about how loud the music is played in an environment which certainly lacks the space (sound engineers could give better details), what kind of ventilation system they provide for non-smokers, what kind of security they provide for their customers, etc.

Quality has always been second in this kind of industries as many other factors prevail for their existence. People do complaint but service providers get away with it as such entertainment is always made as an option and labelled as sin in many religious practices. This gives them an upper hand to dictate to the customers what they are able to provide and you end up taking what they give.

PART 4

Approaches:
Let's Standardize for Quality

In recent times, the word standardization is quickly linked to ISO, which the International Organization for Standardization based in Geneva, Switzerland. Yes, they are indeed the biggest standard developers in the world (almost 20,000 standards covering various industries). One such standard, which could be applied and needed by all the industries, is ISO 9001, which was first published in 1987 and awaiting its latest version in 2015. It can be called as a horizontal standard because it cuts across any industry. This standard also can be said as the most popular standard of them all as it's the Quality Management System (QMS). As mentioned earlier, everyone anywhere around the globe must have Quality is whatever they do, whether it's at work or in their daily life. No one can ever deny the need for a QMS in their life. Due to the emergence of this popular standard more than 30 years ago, a lot organization in various industries has embarked in a journey towards quality through this standard. Organizations were also pressured by their customers to do so in order to continue supplying. The global certification of ISO 9001 has passed more than a million since 2009. However, the organizations having certified to this popular standard don't necessarily gain the best of quality outcome(s) as they would prefer.

Day in and day out we carry out all kinds of task which becomes the requirements of our job. The commitment can be seen from the completion of a particular task whether ad hoc or routine. On "How" to do the task can be usually quite clear through various types of work procedures based on ISO 9001 requirements. However, the bigger question now would certainly be "How well?" did we actually accomplish the given task? A solid answer to this question is very important as it will point us towards the right path of quality and its improvement. Unfortunately, this approach is not really visible in many organizations out there. They do have certain amount of data which may be presented or sent as reports and that's all. This is where the contribution of statistics ends. There will never be any further analysis to the data and this activity will be repeated again and again whenever required.

An organization certified with ISO 9001 (QMS) will certainly go through various phases of improvement which starts even before the compliance audit by a certification body. It is undeniable that number of QMS implementation such as ISO 9001 takes the wrong turn or reaches a death end due the failure to focus on Quality right from the beginning. In all cases the certificate is what matters. A good certificate handing over ceremony and advertisement in the papers is what people look for since the certificate is only seen as a marketing tool for immediate business.

The actual intentions to establish the QMS must be clear from the beginning; however it's not the case for many organizations as it is just a trend to have this certification. Some heads of the system have it as their Key Performance Indicator (KPI) and treat it in isolation in day to day operations. Even in management meetings,

ISO 9001 is placed as a separate issue for discussion. The QMS is not blended in their day to day operations of the organization. There must be some realization that the systems that run with a QMS will enforce habits that ensure quality and these habits are expected to become norms when practiced. These norms will soon become the quality culture of the organization but then the habits and norms are disrupted by poor understanding of the QMS by the leadership with short term goals.

What is much needed is the visible improvement after the certification process because that will be the motivation to move forward in any business. These visible improvements and its experiences realized by an individual or group are certainly needed to touch their Belief system. Only then the manifestations of the right attitude and behaviours can also be seen. However, these types of improvement are not continuously seen in many ISO 9001 certified companies even after the third year of certification. What is expected at this point is some level of maturity in the Quality Thinking of that organization. There many reasons for this to happen such as different intentions for having the certification such as only to get more business, no shared vision for quality, only certain people find it useful and not all, no strong commitment from the top, dealing ISO 9001 in isolation (not part of the organization's daily operations), standardizing too quickly without capturing the under lying variations and quality problems are seen as the responsibility of quality departments only. These and many more related issues can be the major reasons for the downfall of the journey towards quality in many organizations.

One of the main contributing factors for the many failures in the implementation of the QMS is due to the lack of understanding relating to the non-conformances raised during the internal and external audits. Many heads of the system still view non-conformances as a threat. This is because the non-conformances identified are seen as a measure of poor management contributed by a particular individual including the heads of the system. This lack of understanding can sometimes go over board when it's further linked to year end appraisal or performance of an individual. This kind of deviant teachings can give a very negative impact on the Belief system of an individual or group.

The non-conformances that are generated through the internal or external audits must be seen as a great opportunity to improve the system and become the catalyst for change to happen. In certain cases change can be radical through innovation as well. However, failures to realize this simple matter have created another problem where, people who receive the non-conformances want it to be closed out as soon as possible (with or without proper solutions). This has also lead to closing out a non-conformance without even going to the root cause of the entire issue.

It is undeniable that every non-conformance report raised would certainly require a corrective action. However, what most heads of the system do is just come up with corrections which concluded as corrective action. That is why we tend to find many problems (failure events) keep occurring out there. Both the reasons above can be due the *'static auditing'* which is conducting an audit just as part of another mandatory requirement at a given interval. Whether certified or not with management system audit plays a very vital role in making sure changes, improvements or even innovations takes place in an organization. As the Quality Thinking matures over time, the depth of auditing the management system should evolve to highlight greater opportunities for improvement and innovations in the system. There must be *value added auditing and experiences based auditing* to gauge the how well people have accepted the system positively or otherwise.

One should always realize that the highest price to be paid to the lacking of Quality is life itself. That is why a QMS is put in place in order to create a proactive management system. However people are still finding it a problem to report incidents or near misses, which certainly is a very important experience to avoid further disasters or tragedy to oneself or even others around the globe. Every tragedy or disaster that happens in our surrounding must be taken seriously as each event contributes in one way or another to the well-being of mankind. So, we should always be open to learn as much as possible.

An example of a true incident that happened, whereby an 8 month old baby was killed by the babysitter's husband (23 years old) just because the baby was crying while he was asleep. In this sad tragedy the baby came into this world for a short period just to tell us that weaknesses still do exist in the selection system of babysitters. The baby did contribute here so that better childcare system could be created in order for many other parents and children can live peacefully. Day to day we hear or read many such tragedies, which if investigated further leads to previous similar incidents which were over looked or left unattended to. This is the reason why in a QMS audit any findings of weaknesses in the system require the top management to come up with corrective action and not mere corrections.

While we can learn the weaknesses of our system using the Quality Management System (QMS) auditing tool, we should have also learned about the weaknesses of other available systems utilized by various industries that may relate to ours. **Being proactive isn't just about learning from your mistakes but more importantly learning from other people's mistakes in the immediate circle and around the globe**. We can't afford to make all the mistakes in life ourselves just to learn and improve, life is too short to do so.

So, when we perform the root cause analysis for a nonconformity that surfaced, apart from coming up with the corrective actions, we now should also realize the types of risks it carries so that prevention to a potential future nonconformity can be addressed too. These findings and its solutions must be shared to areas that were not affected yet so that others learn and prevent similar mistakes. This knowledge can be cascaded much faster through the Knowledge Management (KM) system in an organization. If this sounds easy, then the question is "Why aren't we learning from other people's mistake or system weaknesses?" well the reason may be because we have not been taught to learn about such situations. We can certainly have myriad of ideas in implementing quality improvements programs but in order to implement a new quality initiative, cleansing of the environment is a must. We should have a holistic view of the entire matter, but what is found out there is an implementation of initiatives just to please the upper management or just participated by only a certain number of employees.

Let's look into some QMS auditing cases

The lack of awareness in management system audits and its importance always brings about many situations that don't quite add any value but further distances people from the QMS. A lot of times we would hear that people get worried the moment they are notified that the auditors are coming. This fear or the uneasiness solely happens when the management systems don't really work for them but unfortunately they end up working for the system. The analogy is like when you sit in the driver's seat of your own car but the car takes you where it wants to go, while you just hold the steering wheel. This means, you have failed to drive the system.

We must come to the realization that, every time a non-conformance report (NCR) is raised after an audit, it gives the organization an opportunity to improve the system from its current weaknesses. When auditing is conducted, everyone must understand the fact is that the auditor actually audits the system and not the auditee (in which ever designation he or she may be). Unfortunately, this understanding isn't easily seen or accepted just because the 'finger pointing syndrome' or the need for 'scapegoat' still prevails in many organizations out there.

Problems in management systems audit will also occur when numbers of NCRs are linked directly to an organization's Performance Measure System (PMS). This is where people end up getting into arguments and so on just to avoid getting any NCRs or else their personal or departmental performance will be affected. At times, we also have PMS that are linked to individual monetary recognition and so on. All this becomes a major hindrance to improvement and innovation through the management system auditing.

When an organization goes for certification in ISO 9001, initially what the internal or external auditors look for is just compliance to the management system that has been established. Development of the QMS at this point is quite easy as everything happens as status quo. All they have to do document whatever they are doing and comply with it. *However, these types of compliance auditing tend to remain a bit too long and systems become rather static. I call this management system audit as an Output Based Auditing.* What happens is that the people become happy by merely achieving the outputs of an executed procedure. Some organizations also prepare a model checklist for their internal auditors and this is used every time audit takes place. So much so, the auditees even know what the auditors are looking for and end up just preparing those matters without fail. This scenario is an example of an internal management system audit going wrong and there's no value added to the existing system at all.

As the organization matures over time after the initial compliance audit, the auditing methodology should evolve as well. Here, auditor's competency should move from Output Based Auditing to Outcome Based Auditing. This means we should be able gauge the performance of the management system through various processes to create the right outcome(s) as expected from the beginning. So, there's a need here to slowly move beyond the procedures and records, by paying more attention to the results that have been achieved. The experiences of the users of the system and recipients of the product or services are also important. Again, this is because it should touch their belief system in the right way so that the system can continue to function for them and not the other way around.

Another problem in QMS auditing is the lack of knowledge among the decision makers when it comes to proposing corrective actions. There are some heads of systems out there don't even understand between Correction, Corrective Action and Preventive Action. There's even situation where none of it is done when a corrective action is requested. Here are a few cases that we can see weaknesses of a QMS auditing:

Auditing and QMS cases 1

The auditor, when inspecting the fridge where vaccines and other types of medicine which require low temperature such as between 2-8 ^0C, found that the min max thermometer gave a maximum reading of 12 ^0C. So, the auditor raised a non-conformance (NCR) on that matter. However, when looking at the proposed corrective action written by *the auditee, it was rather shocking to see that the corrective action was merely a statement from the head of the system telling that "the problem has been solved and it was due power failure. The power supply is back to normal and thanking the auditor for highlighting the problem". That was it, and making the situation worst, the auditor also closed out the NCR without hesitation as he also found the power supply was back to normal and the fridge was functioning well.*

If we study the case above very carefully, you will find that there was no correction, corrective action and how would expect a preventive action. This is due to the lack of understanding among the heads of systems. What should have been done? This usually happens also because the heads of systems don't usually get exposed to any training or workshops related to QMS. They find themselves doing more important things than getting educated on these matters.

What should have been done in the first place and so on is as below:

1. Correction – remove those medicines that cannot be used anymore.
2. Corrective Actions – connect the fridge to an Uninterrupted Power Supply (UPS).
3. Preventive Actions – make sure all other such fridges in other parts of the organization are connected to the UPS.

That's the way to do it and not otherwise. The most important thing here is, we made a mistake due to the weaknesses in the system, we have learned, created a better system and moved on. That is all required whenever a NCR is raised, and not find fault in people. All types of NCRs should be received with an open heart by the respective auditees.

Auditing and QMS cases 2

In the medical diagnosis process at the hospitals, one requirement could be getting samples from patients and sending it to the lab for testing as requested by the doctor. So, samples taken from which ever part of the patients are received at the lab and proceed to the relevant section for testing or sent outside to a bigger lab as services are not available at the present place. The common practice is when the results of the lab test is obtained, they are put in the pigeon holes which represents various wards, units, other smaller hospitals and clinics at district level. This means the job of the lab technicians has ended here (at least that's what they believe). The results of various requests within or outside the hospital will be sitting in the pigeon holes until a representative comes to collect it.

What they fail to realize is that the minute the sample is taken; the patient goes into anxiety mode, thinking whether everything is going to be alright or otherwise. It's an undeniable fact that too much of anxiety (in a negative way) can also kill. As this is related to how the mind thinks of the current situation, the delay in knowing the results is certainly going to create an impact on the patient. The delay in getting the results to the doctor who requested the test is also going to disrupt the care plan for the patient. What kind of experiences has the system created for the patient so far?

This type of practices can also be seen for patients who have regular visits to the specialists' clinics, where the patients come there periodically through pre-arranged appointments. In this situation again request may come from a doctor to take relevant samples from the patient for testing. So, the same processes are followed and this time the results will be kept in the patient files until the next appointment. Patient will only know the results during their next follow up visit; they will be no effort to convey the content of the results unless it is deemed abnormal. Again going back to the fact about anxiety, we tend to fail again to create the positive experience for patient.

Please do understand, this will go unnoticed by the QMS auditors as they believe that the people at the lab have followed the written procedures. So, whatever that the lab technicians or the lab management did was correct to their eyes. Again, it's not wrong to say that the QMS auditors have not evolved from compliance based auditing to a performance and experience based auditing. This is a clear case of lack of customer focus; we should be able to imagine the type of experiences created through this poor system. As I always say, any weak system will have its victim and I believe you can see it here.

Auditing and QMS cases 3

All lecturers at a Vocational Higher Learning Institutions must keep an individual Teaching and Learning (T&L) file for all subjects that are being taught at the institution. In that file, we are able to see the lesson plans, attendance records of the class, academic calendar, class timetable, various assessment results, copy of Medical Certificate (MC) if students are absent for medical reasons, etc. The case here began when procedures indicated that every student must provide evidence if they were absent due to medical reasons, so MCs must be provided to the lectures. This means if the students have been taking seven subjects taught by seven different lecturers, the students will have to provide seven copies of such evidence.

Let's look at one case where a married pregnant woman (student) at the institute had to take a day off to go for her regular check-up and this is considered a medical leave. So, the student had to make copies of the ultra-sound images of her baby and give to her lectures as a record of being absent to the class. Yes, it may sound ridiculous, but this was what happened. Here we can see how much of misinterpretation happens and by doing what they did, in the process violating many other requirements. That kind information above should be kept confidential and not floating around in the T&L file, which can be accessed by anybody apart from the lecturer.

Here we can see the type of experiences created by the weak system for a student who is going through some tough time. One must realize that any good (QMS will never and should never ever jeopardize the Quality of Life of an individual. A QMS such as ISO 9001, will always tell you 'What' all to be done in order to achieve Quality but never at any point tell you 'How" to do it. So, for the case above it's a very clear case of following procedures blindly. I always have been telling people that **when a procedure is written wrongly, without considering the types of variations, the output or the outcomes, people will just do all the wrong things very correctly**.

Auditing and QMS cases 4

In businesses out there, there'll come time where we'll outsource certain processes for ease of managing and probably the cost is much cheaper to do so. However, the sole responsibility to monitor the entire process end to end still lies within the organization that purchased such services. In many instances we came across process owners who claim that they have no information on what's going on as the process is outsourced. This is where things get out of hand and expect things being not the way it was intended to be.

During a QMS audit of an organization which was handling about 20 Haemodialysis machine, meant for renal failure patients, there was an individual waiting to conduct a routine machine servicing. So, we requested the Head of that Department (HOD) to show us some details of that person as he came from a supplier (outsourced services). While the HOD knew where this guy came from, he was unable to tell us who was that individual whom was about to meddle with a lifesaving machine which totally belongs to his department. Again, people fail to draw a clear line of responsibility and accountability when it comes to this kind of matters. Even when asked about the machine itself, such the maintenance record, they were unable to give a precise detail on what has been done thus far. This is not at all good as outsourcing does not mean that whole bulk of the job is handed over to an outside entity that may not have any interest but the dollars and cents.

At this point, what should be understood is that we must be at least sure about the competence and competency of any individual who is going to meddle with such equipment. What the HOD needed to show was that he or she has the details of the person who walked into their system at that point in time. While, it's a security matter on one side, it also gives us the assurance that the outsourced process is well under control. What is expected here is that the organization and the supplier create a partnership that will lead to a better understanding of the organization's objectives in achieving Quality at all times.

I've always been advocating that, one way to create a holistic experience for customers and achieve Quality is by making sure that all interested parties are taken care of at all times. It's always not about what they (suppliers) should do for the money we spent on them but also what we must make sure from our side (the organization) that will allow them to do this without them failing.

Yes, failure at their side is certainly going to create unwanted events on our side as well.

All of the cases above gives us a clear indication that many organizations out there get certified to ISO 9001 (QMS) for the sake of being in the league. They actually don't realize the benefits of this proactive system in ensuring quality output and outcomes. The system they build doesn't work for them but they have to work for the system and this becomes a burden (negative experiences created). QMS audits must be seen as the mover of the system, so that the dynamism of quality can be captured at all times. However, every time the auditor comes, they are seen as fault finders (negative experiences probably also created by the incompetent auditors). As mentioned earlier, the non-conformances (NCRs) that are raised plays an important part in producing new relevant systems and it also creates opportunities to innovate for improvement. This could only happen if we investigate an NCR up to its root cause and provide a robust solution. There should be leaders who find fault on their followers and want those NCRs to be closed out as soon as possible so that it doesn't escalate to the next level. These are leaders who just want to keep their bosses (policy makers) up there happy and show that they (leaders) are still doing a good job managing down below. In reality this has caused a lot of problems to the people within the system as well as the recipient of the product or services of that organization (both government and private).

PART 5

Successful or Not: Are we measuring the right things right?

Numerous processes in an organization are created through many smaller activities which are interlinked. These interacting processes will eventually form the system in an organization within and also how this organization links with other systems outside. In many situations, we find that it's rather difficult for individuals to get the holistic picture of why the organization existed in the first place. This is due to the fact that they are so confined to their processes or even just the smallest activities they take part in.

If someone doesn't understand why that a particular organization, department, section or a unit was formed or existed in the first place then the people involved will never be able to execute whatever task given in the best way possible. I've also noticed that a lot of activities that goes on within a process are carried out without hesitation as it's already written in the procedures. Then there are situations where things are done but it's not written anywhere. They just do it because their predecessors did it, the thought here is, and since it worked for them it should work the same at present time too. Another situation would be when some new ways of doing things is found to be easing the activity but again never documented as the method becomes unique to an individual, so that method goes through a natural death when the person leaves.

Process improvement can and should happen at all times. Any improved processes indicate that people have learned from mistakes and willing to share with others. This will allow the dynamism of Quality to continue at all time. No system shall remain static when Quality is a dynamic phenomenon. There must be a strong belief that we did good yesterday, will do better and achieve the best today.

When talking about activities within a process, there's always chances of us creating tasks that, if we studied carefully will never seem to add any value to the entire process. It was being carried out because it has always been that way or was created out good will, to help someone get another job done faster. Let's look at this scenario where an order form is received from a particular department and while processing the details at the procurement department, the officer in charge had to call back to ask clarification on certain things. This becomes a norm and after acceptance, it becomes a culture. This activity of calling the department adds no value at all to the entire process, however it definitely adds up to the Hidden Cost of Quality. These activities can be called as Non Value Added Activity (NVAA).

The NVAA can happen due to two main reasons:

1. The activity becomes irrelevant due to changes that occur politically, economically, socially, technological enhancements, legally or environmentally. These kinds of changes must be expected at all times in this fast

moving world. As mentioned earlier Quality is a dynamic phenomenon.

2. The other contributor to this kind of situation would be the Failure Event that occurs on a day to day basis like the example above. It's a known fact that a single failure event can lead to the creation of many NVAA. This type of NVAA will disappear when the failure event has been rectified.

So, if we are able to manage any type of NVAA, there is clear opportunity to reduce the hidden cost of quality at all times. These kinds of costs are usually absorbed as the cost of operation and remain hidden in organizations where NVAA activities are accepted as norms. So, the real costs of doing business are always alleviated to a point far from reality. People should always embrace change for the right reasons and not to be too proud about the procedures and work instructions that exist. We don't need the 'Legacy Syndrome' to prevail at any point. *So, are we still measuring the right things out there? Are the measures providing the truth or just some feel good statistics?* What is perhaps the most obvious reason for data collection is to cater to some required daily, weekly, monthly, quarterly or annual reports. Most of the time it's done so routinely that the facts don't change time after time and reporting made easy with the cut and paste mentality. Data is collected and at times without proper supervision or control and sent to another unit or section who will prepare a report (again with the previous template). The content of the reports at time will never have any statistical analysis but drowned with presentation of various colourful graphs and charts that does not add value. Addition to this the over use of percentages to confuse the whole thing. Percentages can mislead if it's not presented in the right way. Let's look at two different examples below:

1. 50% of the Indian population in a small town called Kapit, Sarawak (Malaysia) have left. That really sounded alarming, but the total population was only 2, which means only one guy left the scene.
2. 6.1% of the population of the People's Republic of China live below the poverty line (2013). Sounds small right? But the actual number can be as big as the population of another country and that should be more alarming.

So, use percentages wisely and with the right intention at all times, otherwise people will still remain confused with it.

Many organizations that I've been to have tons of data which they merely compile and present for the many required reports, that's all. There is no further statistical analysis done to understand the trend or any kind of hidden information that can be very vital for better decision making. Another problem is relating to the "Legacy Syndrome" mentioned earlier, the data being collected and the way it's presented remains the same till today. There's poor realization that due to changes in the current world today, some of the data and the methods of analysis may no longer be suitable at this time. When it's clear that there are changes in technology, social engagements and lifestyles, we must be collecting new types of data which may have not been thought of or collected before.

In this modern world it's an undeniable fact that we are exposed to all kind of data. Which of this data can be useful to us? It would depend on our own interest, our background, our nature of job, our lifestyle and so on. Of course the mode of getting it also depends on where we are in the society. The ones who are still IT illiterate would find this data and other information in the main stream media such as paper, TV, radio and so on. Again this does not deter them from gaining the relevant information through people within their circle who may be exposed to level of IT needed to gather such information.

Sometimes too much of irrelevant data could also lead us to making the wrong decisions. That is why, it is rather important to identify all the relevant data and the right information required in a particular situation. For instance how much the fishermen must know before they leave the shores to do their job, how to obtain it, how fast should it reach them, who is responsible in disseminating all this, what are the recent events that should be shared and many more. However, there should be a limit to all these data and information as too much may not help. It's all about the right data and information for the right person, at the right place, at the right time, the right amount and also using the right mode. Failing which it may lead us to disaster or repeated unwanted events.

Any data can be seen as important depending on what issue is it all about. Useful data and its information to one person may not be important to others, so understanding of these variations is also very vital. If we don't have the right measures to a situation, we may never know whether the variations are under control. Dynamism of this relevant data is what we will use as the feed to create dynamic systems which in return leads to a sustainable controlled condition with desired outcomes. Having all this data and dealing with them in isolation will also lead us nowhere.

When we collect data whether it's historical or real time, it must be understood why it's being done in the first place. It's about understanding the difference between needs and wants. There must be clear objectives on data collection, so that right data with rightful amount can be captured. There must be a realization that this data will be analysed to make decisions for the future. This is what makes the whole situation all the more important because any mistakes at this point will lead us to making the wrong decisions.

If are able to capture the right data, only then we can measure the right output and also the desired outcome much later (this is where the establishment of Key Result Areas (KRAs) and Key Performance Indicators (KPIs) come into play, within sustainable controlled condition). The main problem here is the inability to see things as a holistic system. When this prevails, we will view matters in isolation, thus a lot of interrelated data to go missing. This missing link may be the key to may answers that go unanswered even after an investigation or corrective actions have taken place. Due to the fact that different agencies are responsible in handling different matters at the same time, which is further contributed by the bureaucratic nature of the systems implemented, this also leads us to many dead ends. While we may think that it is necessary for control of processes within a system, yet many unwarranted variations could not be explained and of course not forgetting the grey area surrounding the level or types of jurisdiction that the matter is bound by.

One case that can be seen as an example in this kind of matters is when we read about the statistics provided by the traffic police regarding the road accidents that happened. Since they are one of the first to the scene of an accident, numerous identified data are gathered for their reporting needs. After that, another set of data is gathered at another area which is of course the hospital, where it could from the bodies received or injured people at the Accident and Emergency (A&E) of a hospital. This report would give us information on the type of injuries and also what caused the death. These two parts of the information just sits there, isolated from the manufacturer of the vehicles that were involved in the accident.

"In 1927, when Volvo founders Assar Gabrielsson and Gustaf Larson drew plans for their first motorcar, they believed that good design must include the utmost consideration for safety. Their commitment to safety has endured, and has been embraced and expanded today in Gothenburg, Sweden, headquarters of Volvo Cars. Through the years, Volvo has designed safety features based on extensive research of real-world accidents.

In 1970, we formed the Volvo Accident Investigation Team to study accidents involving Volvos. Since then the team has researched more than 20,000 individual accidents, resulting in significant improvements in automobile safety design, many of which have since been adopted by other carmakers. We are proud of this tradition, and hope that our innovations continue to inspire higher standards of safety throughout the automobile industry (www.volvocanada. com., 2009)."

Many similar issues like above is still out there, as long the interrelated agencies don't come together and still perform whatever that they have to in isolation, thus people may never see any desired results within the stipulated timeframe.

The Need for Measurement and Monitoring

Whatever we plan to manage firstly there must an effort to measure the current situation. People from various types of organizations, still fail to understand the importance of measurement. Till today any ideas related to measuring something is considered as extra work. One possible reason for such occurrences could be due the failure in creating the awareness among people on why measurement is needed in an organization. Another reason is also because of the believe that management has proof to blame those responsible for any negative events that took place in the organization. So, even though there is lot of data available, but still its utilization to gain further information is still very minimal. It is just not enough to pile up or back up large amount of data for reference purpose. Organizations must realize that the data they keep has other valuable information as well, if they are explored further.

Measurement can take many forms; depending on the situation it's being used. The idea of measuring has been there for very long time. The proof of the existence of measurements can be found in many civilizations from various parts of the world in different time periods. Evidence is certainly available relating to the expression of a measurement in a number language employs a skill that can be traced back to primitive man.

No one can deny the importance of past records. All the experience gained from previous settings in an organization and the user's experience as well can be employed in current and future settings of the same organization. **Experiences increases knowledge strengthens Beliefs either positively or negatively which further influences the attitude and behaviours**. A well-defined data collection system should be in place at all times. All data and analysis must be fed back on the design and operations, so that necessary corrective action can be planned and implemented as quickly and as economically as possible. Data that is being captured should be from both the desired results and failure events that take place in an organization. Such measurement and continuous monitoring can lead us in making timely decisions in business than can either reduce the failure events which in return may increase the positive events. So, we are also looking at how failure events should be seen for better corrective actions, solutions to various uncertainties, variations and for more positive outcome(s).

Measuring Cost of Quality (COQ)

We talk a lot about cutting costs here and there, in order to make more in bad times or more profit in good times as well. The thing that we must be worried about, are the poor decisions that people make in the name of cutting costs. There are situations where they fail to realize and see the bigger picture of the decisions they made, like for example organizations find that cutting the overtime pay of a worker to reduce costs as times are bad. What indirect costs that they may create in this kind of situation are not taken into consideration at all. In this kind of scenario, the worker's motivation will definitely be effected (as they could have been dependent on that additional income). So workers may just do what they are asked to do not beyond that, which means chances of production delays and drops in productivity may also happen. In the process of cutting costs, what people are capable of doing is creating more Hidden Cost of Quality (HCOQ) with or without realization of the mistake. A person who has a narrow view of a particular situation will tend to take the easy way out by first touching on the pay of an employee, training budgets, claims, bonuses and even the little increments, rather than looking at it holistically. If taking away all these become the first step of recovery, it also means we are taking the problems even deeper to begin with.

What I am trying to say here is that, there are so many other ways to reduce costs, it's not just by looking at the surface, because there are more things hidden below just like the iceberg. These attempts to reduce costs should not only happen when things go wrong but it should be a culture to understand HCOQ in a particular organization. When we come across failure events, we will certainly react to it and when that happens, we will be generating many non-value added activities (NVAA) as mentioned in earlier sections. These activities don't happen for free, we will still be paying for it.

However, many people out there never realize this fact and assume that these happenings are just part of their job. That's the reason why, these types of costs remain hidden at all times.

Until the 1950s this concept had not been extended to the quality function, except for the departmental activities of inspection and testing. Quality related costs were scattered among various accounts, especially "overhead" accounts. Over the decades as more studies done, some surprises emerged, that is the quality related costs were much larger than had been shown in the accounting reports.

Where does the HCOQ come from? Well, the hidden money comes from the Cost of Poor Quality (CoPQ). The CoPQ of an organization is the money that we pay when things go wrong; when failure events emerge, NVAA are generated. When this happens we will have to pay for time lost, additional charges and material wastages. Unfortunately, as mentioned earlier all these types of costs are not easily seen or captured by the regular accounting system. What happens here is that these costs are absorbed as the operating costs or the cost of doing business. This is why; it's kind of hard to believe the annual financial report of an organization that gives us the Profit Before Tax (PBT) or Profit After Tax (PAT).

Based on table below, we can say that this is the common scenario that takes place in many organizations. Here the focus is on the hidden failure costs. It is clear that Profit = Revenue - Cost of doing Business but the issue that many people ignore is that the cost of doing business consist of the **hidden failure costs** apart from the **visible failure costs**. This hidden failure costs is usually added into the operational costs. One main reason is because it is assumed to be very difficult to quantify these kinds of costs. People will have to realize that a single failure event that takes in an organization will generate many NVAA. These activities will further generate both visible and hidden failure costs. So, the real cost of doing business will always be overestimated when we fail to capture, reduce or eliminate the hidden failure costs. Based on various studies and reports, the CoPQ can range from 5 percent and up to 50 percent of an organization's the revenue. This very much depends on the types of industry and also whether being in the private or government sector.

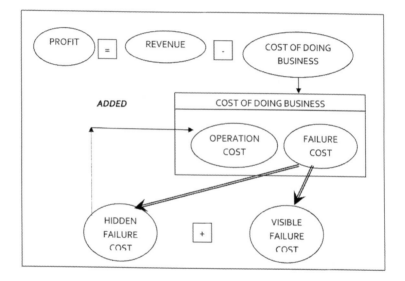

Categories of COQ (PAF Model)

These categories COQ was established in the mid-1950s by Dr. Armand Feigenbaum (April 6, 1922- November 13, 2014) an American Quality Guru and a businessman.

- Internal Failure Costs – these are costs associated with defects that are found prior to transfer of the product to the customer. They are costs that could disappear if no existed in the product prior to shipment.

- External Failure Costs – these are costs associated with defects that are found after product is shipped to the customer. These costs also would disappear if there were no defects.
- Appraisal Costs – These are cost incurred to determine the degree of conformance to quality requirements.
- Prevention Costs – These are costs incurred to keep failure and appraisal costs to a minimum.

However, do take note that when we talk about the HCOQ, we mainly refer to the extension of internal and external failure costs as categorized by Dr.Feigenbaum.

The Way to Look at a Failure Event

Based on the table below, we must understand that one failure event will certainly generate many Non-Value Added activities (NVAA). Since every failure event will certainly trigger many NVAA, it is vital for an organization to identify, understand and eliminate them. Another important reason why we should look into all these failure events is because it's actually mistakes that are already been made, so with this information there is *a very good opportunity for us to learn from other people mistakes and not waste our lifetime making all the known mistakes ourselves*. We often find that people also react to failure events as if it's unique, but in most cases it may just be a repetitive event which occurred at a different time, day, place or even involving different people.

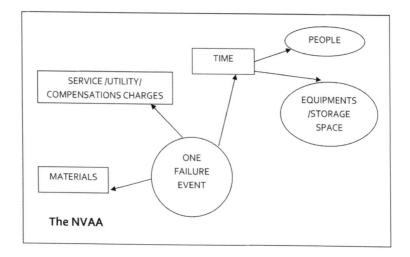

The NVAA

Failure Events Layout from an Organizations Perspective

Let's go back to the famous quote by Crosby "Doing it Right the First Time", this means if we are able to do it right the second time, we will still be paying the price of Non-conformance for the first failure event. So, we can't deny that any failure event don't come for free. Every failure comes with a price, which is known as the Cost of Poor Quality (CoPQ). That's why the famous Quality Guru Philip Crosby said Quality is Free (his best seller book back in 1979) if you do it right the first time. By the way monetary loss can always give greater attention from the relevant parties. **Philip Crosby,** (June 18, 1926 – August 18, 2001) was a businessman and author who contributed to management theory and quality management practices.

We can see that failure costs can affect an organization in three possible ways i.e., before, during and after a product or service is delivered (that includes Q3, from phases transformation of Quality from specification to experiences). The classifications are further explained below:

1. AEFC (Anterior External Failure Cost) - these costs will occur from the poor management of the suppliers or external service providers. The problems that usually occur are delay in deliveries, material and/or specification defects, wrong delivery, selection of the wrong or incapable external service providers, limited suppliers, incompetent suppliers, poor outsource management control, lack of partnership and so on. Failure to capture this cost can lead to further unnecessary problems, which means generation of more internal failure costs. *Educating any external service providers or suppliers of an organization regarding the needs to reduce these types of costs has to be a priority to create a sustainable all win (every single interested party) partnership.*

2. IFC1 (Internal Failure Cost 1) - these are costs that will occur when there is poor planning, organizing and ineffective decisions. These can be problems such poor leadership in terms of vision and commitments, creation of a bad system (not working for the people but the individuals have to work for the system, QMS), poor documentation of systems, branding policies, internal and external education policies (all interested parties), poor knowledge management policies, poor understanding of risks and risks appetite, poor management and maintenance of infrastructure policies, Human Capital policies, poor measurement and monitoring policies (sometimes irrelevant at this time), and so on. These costs can be very much hidden as planning, organization and decisions are made by 'high ranking' people in the organization. These costs can't be detected in a very short period and at times it may come to light only

when there's a change in organization's leadership and its systems. *Do take note that leadership is pretty much pulled into this costs because it involves policy matters.*

3. IFC2 (Internal Failure Cost 2) - these are costs that is due to interruptions that may occur during the daily management of operations of an organization. Any individual in the organization regardless of positions held can encounter problems due to operation matters. The interruptions can be due to poor dealings with external service providers or suppliers, malfunctioning computers or machine breakdowns due to poor maintenance, procedures not followed, having to queue for the Photostat machine, poor results, reworks, scraps and the list goes on and on. Even though these types of problems occur rather frequently but usually they are accepted as a norm (that soon becomes a culture) and also considered as a minor problem. However, if studied in depth, there will be a lot of non-value added activities (NVAA) caused by a certain failure event. Most people fail to understand that these so-called minor problems can create a very large amount of waste (monetary) due to the frequency of its occurrence.

4. PEFC1 (Posterior External Failure Cost 1) - these are poor quality cost that can occur during and after delivery of a product or service. These costs can also be intangible in certain areas. There are also some costs that can be quantified with easily available data such as warranty claims, poor inspection and testing (high reliance on it can also inflate the costs), number of wrong delivery, poor handling of storage, distribution, delivery and packaging that caused damage, poor marketing and product or service education, unsuitable brandings (irrelevance), incompetence, loss of opportunity and so on. Even though

there are some easily quantifiable costs from this part but they are also left unnoticed in some organizations.

5. PEFC2 (Posterior External Failure Cost 2) - these are costs that a customer has to face or even may be facing during or after a warranty period (mainly focused on the experiences that touch the belief system of an individual). These are costs that a customer has to pay after he or she had the product or service provided, which is certainly caused by the knock on effects from the all four types situations mentioned above. The usual type of costs can be transportation costs for making warranty claims, making calls for further technical help due to faulty products or service, costs of time wasted resolve the problem. Perhaps another large portion that is often not considered is the cost of damage, be it to life or property (death caused by product or services rendered, example airbags in car explodes, bridge collapsing, food poisoning, cracks in buildings, leaking pipes and many more) due to the failure of the product or service to deliver the expected result. Many customers have suffered the consequences with little or no recourse on the matter. So, there will be further loss of opportunities and creation of a bad image for the organization that provided the product or service. This may be the most difficult poor quality cost to quantify. However there's also a very little effort to quantify these costs. Experiences created from this part certainly will create the right or wrong perception towards the Quality of a product or service. Belief systems of individuals will be touched with the right or wrong reasons as well.

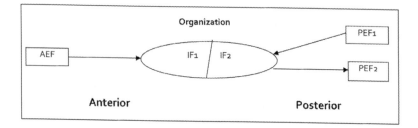

A Common Scenario

Let's look at a scenario when a customer makes a complaint. Firstly, we must understand that a customer complaint is failure event. As mentioned earlier, this failure event would trigger some activities that can be non-value-added for both internal and external customer satisfactions. So, all the non-value-added activities that are attached (usually hidden) to this failure event is as below:

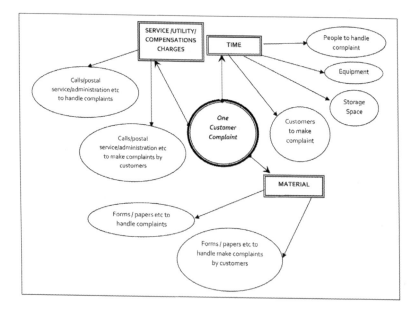

Based on table above, we can get a clearer picture on how the elements of waste which was explained in earlier section can be generated by the occurrence of a single failure event (customer complaint). These NVAA that are usually triggered to correct the situation which went wrong and certainly do not add value for both internal and external customers. While, many reasons are given for not quantifying the hidden and visible failure costs, it must be noted that it is something very much required in any problem solving agenda. The accurate amount and the frequencies of its occurrence can be the base for building a good Business Case of a particular problem that must be resolved. *Do refer to the paper titled "Increasing the visibility of the hidden failure costs" in the Measuring Business Excellence – The journal of organizational performance management (Volume 10, Issue 4, 2006), to get a clearer understanding on the method of calculating the hidden failure cost of quality.*

PART 6

Quality of Teaching and Learning

People are involved in all kinds of roles and responsibilities in their day to day working life. While these roles can be created to suite the job and designations given, the actual competency needed is sometimes still not clear. When asked how long it takes to have a minimum or acceptable level of competency in order to carry out the job, the common answer is, it depends on the person involved. If they learn fast, it will quick otherwise it will take time. They can never seem to give an absolute time frame for attaining the required minimum competency to perform the task without supervision. This is something that should not be accepted as an answer at all. When we hear this kind of answers, it clearly shows that the individual is not properly inducted into the system and to do so there isn't any clear mechanism to create the level of competency needed. Again, going back to the weaknesses of the system, as I always say, if the system is weak it will certainly create a victim. These victims could be people within the system, involved in various interrelated processes or a man on the street that depend on such systems provided by the organization.

When we talk about competency, one fails to realize that it involves many components such as knowledge, experience, skills, aptitude and attitude. There's always a tendency to blame on one glaring component which is the attitude. The problem is, it's an interrelated factor, so it should be looked in depth to get a clearer picture of each component above. It is certainly easy to point at attitude and rest the case but one should see beyond that. As we discussed earlier, what is shaping this type of attitude and behaviour? What kind of belief system that was created in the first place?

To ensure quality outcomes at all times, there must be a strong emphasis in the part of teaching and learning in an organization. An organization that don't give the rightful priority to the teaching and learning of its employees, will certainly find it difficult to cope with the rapidly changing environment. In this current time providing the basics of training alone isn't enough, the organization's leadership must be totally committed in ensuring teaching and learning takes place.

The common scenario when it comes to teaching and learning in an organization is by asking the Heads of Departments (HODs) to propose the kind of training deemed needed after some internal evaluation and intuition. These lists of training requirement are then given to the Human Resources or Training Department to arrange those requested. These training may be done internally if the resources available or outsourced to external service provider. However, it should be realized that teaching and learning can happen in many ways, but the important thing is also to see whether it's happening at the right time and place for an individual requiring a particular competency. If we fail to impart the right knowledge and ensure competency at the right time, we will certainly create many victims through this poorly managed system.

Every single individual in an organization or in their daily life have various responsibilities, so competency is vital in ensuring that the given tasks gets done within a specified time. It's natural that we need to continuously learn new things (knowledge) and new way of doing things (skills) all the time. So, what is needed is an environment that gives the right experiences to encourage learning. The leadership of an organization play a very important role to ensure that continuous learning happens through the organization regardless of individual's roles and position. This is because ensuring quality outcomes is everyone's responsibility.

People may also have difficulty in learning; this variation must also be understood clearly, so that the right teaching and learning mechanism can be put in place to encourage learning. Again, as we pointed out earlier, failure to capture the smallest variation of a situation may lead us to negative experiences that will impact the belief system of an individual in the wrong way.

Leaders must also change their leadership styles from just directing and giving orders to a more coaching approach. They must play a pivotal role in the teaching and learning of employees in an organization. This is because it's not about the qualification an employee already have but how to enhance the current competency of an employee so that they can contribute enough for the organizational excellence. In order to do so, *every employee must be provided with a dynamic learning roadmap which will ensure that no one is left behind in the ever changing environment.*

Total Quality can only be achieved if we are able to approach things holistically and definitely not through isolated adventures. The same goes for teaching and learning in an organization. The teaching and learning that takes place in an organization must further relate to all interested parties, which include suppliers, other agencies, customers, etc. The organization must take the responsibility to educate all the interested parties that they are dealing with. This will be an important advantage to the organization as there will a mutually beneficial relationship with all parties involved.

All teaching and learning in an organization must be structured and planned well; even if it's an ad hoc need. We often hear methods such as On the Job Training (OJT) or the mentor mentee approach in ensuring competency in an organization. However, in some organizations these methods became a technique that leads to **'probable learning'**, as it depends solely on the mentor (teacher) and circumstances of the day to create the learning experience. This is should never be case for any attachment with the mentor regardless of the work related situation on that day or the mentor's personal problems. In order do have a proper teaching and learning experience that ensure the needed outcomes, a structured module must be created an followed very stringently. Whatever we discussed so far, it isn't about the people in the organization alone but all the interested parties as mentioned earlier.

Let's us take a common scenario which relates to ensuring competency; Do take note that Competence is a person's ability, skills and knowledge that he or she possesses with the right attitude and aptitude thus far. However, Competency is the skills required to perform the job (the same job can have variations in executions due to new environment, new methods, new types customers, new equipment and infrastructure). That's the reason it's very important to ensure competency no matter how old the person may be doing the same job in other places.

When auditing a cryogenic lab that's stores cord blood in a special storage tank, it was found that the cord bloods were stored with liquid nitrogen at a temperature of minus 190 degree Celsius. Umbilical cord blood is blood that remains in the placenta and in the attached umbilical cord after childbirth. Cord blood is collected because it contains stem cells, which could *be used to treat haematopoiesis (process of production, multiplication, and specialization of blood cells in the bone marrow) and genetic disorders. Since, this lab provides a more specialized service compared to normal labs and the work place hazards are at different level, so competency of the lab technician is very important. When we asked the supervisor on how he or she ensures competency of the new lab technician (even if someone is competent with many years of experience working in labs), the simple answer was that there is a 8 weeks structured module for On the Job Training (OJT). The new lab technicians will be mentored by an assigned supervisor based on the module and only be able to work alone after certified through the 8 weeks program. Due to the fact that the new staff never works alone, at least for the first 8 weeks, the chances of mistakes or creating victims in the system isn't that easy.*

The next scenario can happen if the suppliers are not in the organization's teaching and learning loop:

I was at a talk and the coffee break was at 10:30am, so when we came out the tea or coffee served was already cold. When asked, why the drinks were cold? The caterer replied the coffee break was scheduled at 10:00am and we came out late. This clearly shows that the organization failed to educate the supplier on the requirements of providing the right quality of service for this organization. However, since we gave a feedback at that time, at the next coffee break a flask that could contain heat was used by the supplier. That was certainly a quick action and was much appreciated by all the customers. These little things are the ones that make the greatest difference. The experiences gave everyone a more positive view towards the supplier and their ability to serve. It is must be understood here that any feedback provided by the customers or end users on this matter isn't a provision to sack or blacklist the service provider. By ensuring the competency of suppliers in this scenario, we are also able to ensure a beneficial partnership that will satisfy all our interested parties at that point.

Since we have talked a lot about teaching and learning, what type of experiences that should be created in order to have the highest impact on learning? Yes, to answer this question, one of the first things to do is to understand the variations that exist between the learners and their capability of learning. Everyone can be taught and everyone can learn, there's no doubt about that but the variations in the learning capability and capacity at a particular time for an individual must be known. This is important for us to design a proper module with accurate delivery and deployment mechanisms when it comes to teaching and learning.

In order to capture the variations that exist among the learners and provide them a more reliable way of teaching, there's a need for an activity called **Learning Needs Diagnosis (LND)**. This must be conducted to gauge the way an individual or group wants to learn. The learning must be deployed and delivered in the most efficient and effective way possible. When a proper LND is not done, we will certainly go wrong in the delivery and deployment part of the learning solution. So, the training conducted will only benefit a selected few and it won't be holistic enough to be benefited by the organization in terms of Return on Training Investment (ROTI).

At this point, it must be clear that the quality of teaching and learning certainly plays an important part in ensuring the right competency is created for the right individual at the right time. We must always be able to tell about; what is being taught, when it's being taught, the content of what being taught, where (environment) it's being taught, how (methods, tools and techniques) it's being taught and by whom it's being taught (internal resource or external experts). This knowledge will allow each and every individual in an organization to have a clear learning roadmap at all times. This will certainly allow smooth transition if someone leaves the system and another individual takes over a position. *Job handover isn't as easy as what is portrayed where one individual hands over a huge thick book (so called job description) to another individual through a ceremony witnessed by many and not forgetting camera clicking left, right and centre.*

Another interesting scenario that should be noted is relating to retiring. Isn't it a norm when hiring, we always asks for certain level of qualification and certain time period of experience an individual must have acquired. However, the sad part is all that accumulated experiences and competencies become invalid when you reach a specified age of retirement (a terminology used for exiting a system, that's all). What should be noted here is that retired is not equal to expire (dead, gone, no more use). This valuable people are often just forgotten and the organization just loses the wealth of knowledge and experiences held by these individuals who can share it with the current generation through various suitable or applicable teaching and learning mechanisms. However, it must also be noted that there must be a very clear method of selection on who can come back and serve. This is because if we are not careful, we may end up bringing someone who can influence people the wrong way in the name of teaching, which will prove disastrous for the organization.

It's always about what we believe that takes us into the next level of thoughts and action. Of course it's quite difficult to see it from right or wrong and most of the time it depends on the social norms, your personal competency and surroundings. The belief system changes with the levels of exposure we get in certain issues. The exposures a person gets on anything out there, could be by believing what he or she saw, by feeling whatever it may be, personally experiencing it when being there, by just knowing it through other means or even was just an influence by another individual or group. Whatever that shaped that belief system, one thing is for sure it's certainly a dynamic matter. So, the right opportunity should be taken to look into this phenomenon very seriously as many outcomes of various noble efforts depends on it.

PART 7

Innovation: How was it possible?

Besides Quality another buzz word of the decade is definitely Innovation, which is eventually linked to the quality outcomes that creates value. So, as usual everyone talk, use and feel happy being linked to the word innovation and feel good when labelled innovative as well. Innovation as a word isn't new; it can be linked way back to seventeenth century, however it took root as a word in science and industry in the nineteenth century. This also tells us that innovation isn't an economic term after all. Just like Quality (standards for quality assurance was pretty much within armed forces), innovation between 1950s to 1980s was something very much linked to new inventions and confined to processes within labs that bring about commercial products.

*"**Innovation** comes from the Latin innovationem, noun of action from innovare. The Etymology Dictionary further explains innovare as dating back to 1540 and stemming from the Latin innovatus, pp. of innovare "to renew or change," from in- "into" + novus "new".*

So, Innovation can be seen as the process that renews something that already exists and NOT like what people believe that, it's the introduction of something new. ***The point to note is that the*** *meaning of innovation really relates to renewal with novelty.* For this renewal with novelty (the quality of being new, original or unusual) to happen it is vital that people to change the way they think, make decisions, do things differently and be able to make choices outside of their norm. It must be clearly understood that innovation defers from invention, while innovation paves way for renewal with novelty, inventions on the other hand works on the premise to directly create the idea or methods itself (never before existed). *Innovation should also be seen as different from improvements as innovation refers to the notion of doing something different rather than doing the same thing better.* We can see that all this revolves around 3Is (that is Invention, Improvement and Innovation). There is this cycle that every product or service goes through till they hit the last I (that is being Irrelevant, inadequate, inefficient or ineffective). When a product or service is deemed irrelevant, then this calls for the 3Is to come into play to cater the need for change.

Let's look at this example to make it simple:

Alexander Graham Bell, Scottish-born scientist, inventor, engineer and innovator who is credited with inventing the first practical telephone. If we compare the looks, shapes, sizes and combinations of other inventions brought about the various improvements and innovations related to telecommunications devices that we have today. The need for change happens every time the telecommunication devices become irrelevant, inadequate, inefficient or ineffective due to various contributing factors. However, every innovation that is introduced from this invention must also have processes that go through improvements on the day to day basis before they become irrelevant. That is the link between invention, improvement, innovation and irrelevance. All of the changes that happened to the telephone from the inventor's hand to what we see today were contribution of the 3Is in making sure that Quality outcome(s) that add value were achieved at every phase of Quality (Q1 to Q3).

The truth about innovation is, it's not something too difficult that anyone should be afraid of or shy away. However, like many good initiatives out there it's made difficult by the lack of understanding, awareness and commitments from the relevant individuals or groups. Innovation is simply the ability to change the smallest things with novelty that creates value for everyone. A lot of people also believe that innovation needs a lot investment and there must be a tangible product that must be showcased. Again, this is certainly related to inability to understand the difference between innovation and invention. The reality is everyone can be creative and innovative, while providing innovative outputs that create quality outcomes that add value.

Many organizations as usual get excited when there's hype in certain initiatives, and further added sensation is created when supported by the government of the day or it's a global phenomenon that touched everyone. In the present time, all this catches the attention of people too quickly, like the wild fire during the dry season assisted by the wind. The assistance here certainly is the technology and the ability to connect globally at ease, while not forgetting it is real time too. Well, there are pros and cons to this happening, while it's good to be abreast of happenings and be part of it. However, the speeds at times don't allow us to think carefully on what is there to be done. Again, as discussed earlier, something done not looking at the bigger picture and not holistic in its approaches, the outcomes will certainly be below par.

Let's look at a misconception relating to innovation:

When asked an individual on what are the challenges faced in ensuring the innovation culture in their work place, the answer was rather alarming. The individual explained that he was not a scientist to begin with and don't know why all this forced on to him. He claimed further that his background was more to business administration and corporate law. I was taken aback but my immediate answer was "come on, you are creative and innovative all the time, we humans are such creatures. Just imagine all the things that you did at home to make your life as comfortable as possible (create value) in a continuous manner even if your resources are limited. You may have done wonders that were appreciated so much by your loved ones that lead to quality outcomes (i.e. Quality of Life). So, your education background and the field that you are in isn't the measure of being innovative.

Anyone can be innovative at any time and usually the circumstances or the situation will force them to be one. If it was not for the natural instinct to change from one stage to another with novelty, we won't be where we are today. If you look deep into inventions and innovations they have a very strong relationship with nature. A lot of inventions were a reality by looking at how nature works, for instance we saw the birds before inventing the aircraft, we saw a kingfisher (bird) to build a bullet train in Japan, a beetle inspired a fog harvesting surface to collect moisture in arid environment, looked at fish build a car and many more.

Think outside the box: What is it all about?

What is this thinking outside the box all about? What's actually inside that box everyone is talking about? Well, it's actually the basic thoughts of moving away from the norm (which is inside the box). However, these boxes must be seen holistically and not by focusing on one box relating to one individual. When asked about 'how' to think outside the box, then you'll hear answers like go watch a new movie, eat at different places, change your daily routine, do learn about other industries, eliminate negative thinking, surround yourself with positive people, draw a picture, take shower, invite randomness and many more. While, the answers can be inspirational to think creatively towards a solution but we still got to know what box are we looking at and what's in it. It's just like having tool box and assuming that you can repair anything. An individual or group must also have the competency to take out the right tool for a particular problem at hand.

The boxes (at least some of it) that we suppose to think outside from can be consisting of things like:

- Leadership styles – autocratic, bureaucratic, charismatic, visionary, team and many more.
- Individual or group belief system – knowledge, exposure, experiences, habits, attitude and behavior
- Organizational culture – vision, values, habits, systems, symbols, language and so on.
- Work – methods, mechanisms, procedures, work instructions, rules, regulations, protocols, and so on.
- Measurements and control – performance measures, assessments, evaluations and feedbacks.
- Work environment – ambiance, motivation, communication, transparent, teams, recognitions and more.

These are some of the boxes with current conventional practices that you have to think outside of it. When people are very much in comfort within those boxes, then it'll be an uphill task to get people to move towards innovation. However, when there is a powerful enough pressure from within or externally for an individual, group or organization to change, then there will be a need to think outside those boxes. Another thing that will also happen due to the pressure to change is creativity, this is also because resources won't change immediately and may take time. So, people have no choice but to creatively move towards innovation with or without additional resources. To those organizations that have unlimited resources, they may do this in different ways using all available means creatively.

There's always many ways to be creative and innovative as long we gain the right knowledge, skills, exposure, freedom (controlled), resources (even when limited) and pressure to change (internally or externally).

Being innovative requires certain basic things, that is

1. Leadership providing – commitment, collaborations, funding, vision, mission, objectives, freedom to change, infrastructures, safe space for innovation activities and labs
2. realization the need for change (with the right amount of pressure to do so)
3. identifying, understanding and connecting the relevant boxes that we need to think outside from
4. ideation methods that's suitable and accepted by all (with the right working environment and communication channels)
5. get to know the best practices out there(within or external to industry)
6. creating the right collaborations – immediate circle that you are dealing with, the circle that do similar businesses, the circle that you see as a role model (can be outside your industry) and the circle of science an academics.

7. understanding the variations between the boxes and the variation that needs to created (PV)
8. knowing and addressing the consequences that change will bring (UV, risk assessments) – risk appetite
9. measuring the current status of the weaknesses using the right attributes, to measure the same during the solution outcomes
10. enhancing knowledge, exposure and skills with the best methods of teaching and learning. Teaching and learning done creatively to expedite the learning process and subsequent use of the knowledge, exposure and skills (learning agility).
11. recognition and further standardization of the innovation will be motivating factor for sustainability.

When these requirements above are isolated in execution, any innovation will become less effective and required culture will never be formed.

Innovation that can be seen here and there

You must have seen a lot of things from past brought back to the present time with a bit of creative inputs to it and we got a brand new product. One of the usual areas we can see that is in the fashion industry, where old clothing styles are blended with the current environment and new fashion or trend is formed. So, looking into the old books, magazines and papers might bring new innovative ideas to solve a present day problems or needs.

Innovation can be created by generating ideas by looking at the nature, wild imaginations (even from the movies or books), best practices (related or nonrelated) and so on. If you look and think of a new product or services in depth you will notice these few characteristics (vise versa), such as

- old to new
- slow to fast
- big to small
- inside to out
- near to far
- loud to quieter
- less to more
- bright to darker
- long to short
- high to low
- smooth to rough
- soft to hard
- dry to wet
- up to down

Just look at how many products and services out there catered to such needs above in various industries and call it innovation. Come to think of it, it's just too many and that's how innovation works. So, don't get stressed over the need to coming up with an innovative solution for a particular problem or need. Most importantly remember that we have always been innovating and each individual have that capability buried deep inside. All they need is the right trigger and opportunity to bring it out to create wonders.

PART 8

Feedback Management:
Just create the right closure

Any kind of system out there cannot be running the processes and its activities on a 'One Way Street' flow. There should always be a closure in any system made of these processes (the loop must be closed and there shouldn't be any loose ends). What I am talking about here is regarding having and managing Feedback, this mechanism must be embedded in any process right from the input to the outcome stage. There's many ways for us to get feedback from the interested parties of an organization. However, the realization that feedback is needed at all times must be there in order to make sure that an organization's strategic movements towards its vision are not disrupted at any point.

A lot of organization out there can be seen collecting all kinds of feedback from their customers (both internal and external). This could be due to genuine reasons for improvements and serve better. There's also another group of organization that does it for the sake of doing it or just don't want to be left out of the trends of getting feedbacks. As for a feedback it could be a complaint, complement or a comment (the 3Cs). The challenge is how do get them the right way and in a timely fashion.

Yes, we can gather feedback round the clock, every day without fail but how much is it going to help us in our endeavour towards achieving quality. I have had the opportunity to see many feedback mechanisms that are there just to satisfy some requirement somewhere either internally or externally. There has been a poor understanding in this area, which leads to a lot of misinterpretation of the data when analysed or just compiled for reporting and decision making. If mistakes take place from the source of a particular feedback, any further analysis of the data will just be a waste of time.

Feedback can be gathered reactively or proactively, of course the latter would be more preferred, in order to avoid any unwanted situation. However, in many organizations out there, we are able to notice at least the availability of complaint forms (hardcopy or electronically) or a suggestion box at various points. Yes, this is certainly a reactive manner in obtaining feedbacks. While the proactive method would be like a customer satisfaction surveys, interviews, focus groups, etc., where we try to understand where we stand when it comes to providing a product or services.

Feedbacks can be classified into two categories by means of collection point

1. Passive Feedback – where it is reactive in nature and gathered through secondary inputs. These types of information can be gathered from media (all kinds), suggestion boxes, customer complaints forms, etc. Here we wait to get the feedbacks.

2. Active Feedback – where it's a planned proactive way of getting feedbacks through a primary inputs. This can be done through customer satisfaction surveys, interviews, focus groups, open days, etc.

As mentioned earlier, the bigger question is 'how' and 'when' to get the feedbacks.

Here are some cases that would give you an idea of what could go wrong:

- A report was made at the counter of an enforcement agency and after experiencing that process, the client was given a feedback form to rate on how satisfied are they with the services provided. So, data has been collected at any time of the day when the customers walk in to make any report. Here, the organization feels that they have done enough to gather the feedback from their respective client. Unfortunately, they failed to realize that what was gathered is merely an experience at the input level of the service provision and all other levels right up the outcome are left unaccounted for. This is definitely a classic blunder in gathering feedbacks. So, the holistic experience of the client going through various stages of the process is lost.

- In another situation with similar consequences happened at a hospital's 'father friendly delivery room', where immediately after a father experiencing the child birth and his wife going through delivery, the father was given a feedback form to be filled up. While, the experience is still fresh, however we could still find a better time in giving the feedback form. This is because emotionally there will a lot of things running through the father's mind after such an experience, especially if it's for the first time.

- In many situations, there are also tendency to make the wrong selection of samples, which means the criteria for sample selection isn't very clear. One example would be when we are to gather feedback from patients who are admitted in the ward of a hospital. When do they qualify to answer the questionnaire? For instance, the patient who got admitted less than 24 hours can be classified differently and feedback should be gathered in different manner. This because they may not have experienced the holistic service provision. As mentioned earlier if variations between the customers are not identified, any approach will certainly prove futile. Giving the questionnaire to the wrong subject or respondent is as good as not doing the study at all.

- When would be the best time to gather feedback and especially if we are doing it actively. Again, what type of variations must be understood and further classified for data collection. Issues such time of the day, which day of the week, which week of the month or which month of the year are all important factors to be considered when capturing any kind of feedbacks at all times. If we fail to do so, we will certainly end up with an inaccurate data set that will further lead towards a disastrous reporting as well.

- Capturing feedbacks through various mechanisms is certainly possible but inadequately equipped tool will not get us very far as well. We should always understand our intentions on what are we measuring very clearly, otherwise we will never capture the types of experiences a client goes through before, during and after a product or services have been delivered. The designing of the questionnaire or a checklist for interviews must be carefully scrutinized taking into consideration of all the variations and a clear limitation of the study must be established. Only then we are able to analyse, interpret, report and make the right decisions.

- One other area where feedback is not gathered properly is when teaching and learning or training happens (classroom or On the Job). This is also the case with organizations having certified with ISO 9001 that requires the organization to gauge whether there's a difference between before attending a selected course and after. The one thing they always do is collecting feedback at the end of a training session or a program. What captured here is merely on matters relating during and immediately after the course such as whether the learning objectives are met, whether it was taught well, whether presentation was clear, whether the notes given were appropriate, whether the food served during breaks were good, whether the accommodations provided was comfortable and so on. However, while all those information are also important for future programs but another important part of the feedback must come in after a suitable passage of time. This particular feedback must come from the superiors of the system as they can see and evaluate clearly whether the action to send the individual or a whole group for that specific training was worthwhile. After having this information and discussing it in a post mortem or management review meeting, only then the respective file must be closed. The lessons learned will be used to design better future courses by experts within or working with outsourced service providers. Do take note that there are many methods to gauge whether an individual or group have learned well and were able to apply the learning. People just get carried away and always try using a questionnaires but it may not be suitable at times. A simple phone call with structured questions in a checklist could do the job too. The important thing is the valuable data for us to improve further to created quality learning solutions and the right experiences.

These feedbacks that an organization gathers must be timely and it's very important to be discussed in a post mortem or management review meeting. Upon having decided on the lessons learned and the needed action for future projects, only then the files should be closed. This information from the lessons learned should be the feed for any new or similar projects, so that proper planning and allocation of resources can be done with very minimal Unproductive Variations (UVs). These kinds of information are usually kept at the Project Management Office (PMO) or the respective departments that handled the projects.

PART 9

DRSK Framework for Robust Solutions at the end and beyond

Well, life is filled with all kinds of challenges whether at home, at work or even when we are on holidays. One of the main reasons for people not being ready to face those challenges is due to the lack of ability to embrace change. **We can't remain constant with our current system forever when change is a constant phenomenon.** This means new challenges will always be there, it's for us to anticipate the kind of actions needed to address those challenges. So, after understanding what is Quality, Quality Thinking, Variations, Quality Management System(QMS), Innovation, Importance of Teaching and Learning, Auditing that adds value, Competency, COQ, NVAA and Managing Feedback, this will certainly allow everyone to think in a holistic manner when dealing with any problems. In order to ease the process of thinking and finally solve a problem I put forth the DRSK framework for robust solutions. When you or a team is given a task to come up with solutions to address a particular problem, the DRSK framework will certainly be very handy. It's very simple but makes everyone think out any boxes you may be presented with and yet holistically.

Let's now talk about the content of the first letter **D** that represents Demands to Destiny. This part is to ensure that when people are eager to solve a problem now, they should already have the end in mind. The need to change can happen anytime, but doing something in haste without thinking what is there to be realized at the end, will just be a waste of time. This is because it will eventually fizzle out as people were not given the chance to visualize any of the possible outcomes to move towards to. When addressing a single demand/need, it will be linked with a few desired outcomes. So, from the beginning everyone would understand that by addressing the specified demand/need, we are able to realize all those outcomes. This is very important as it gives focus to the team to create a solution that ensures all desired outcomes are realized.

Demands to Destiny	Requirements	Based on
Demand/ Needs	This is what's **needed** to solve a particular problem or to address any requirements. Do address one need at a time.	Strategies, mandate, reports and studies, regulatory requirements, New Policy requirements, Brainstorming (Ideation), Nonconformities from management audits, daily situational problems.
Desired Outcomes	These are the **desired outcomes** that should be realized upon addressing the needs.	Strategies (Short term, Mid-term, Long term), KPIs, the types of problems that will be addressed.

When we are clear with what is needed and all the desired outcomes (the end in mind), only then we can even think about what to do in order to achieve all those outcomes. So, to address this we have the letter **R** which represents Right to Risk. At this point, it must be understood that the organization may already have an existing system in place. Since, there are weaknesses in the system we may want to create a new experience by introducing the PV. However, there could also be situations where the PV being introduced will be something totally new to the organization. Whether the PV is an extension from the current way of doing things or totally new, the chances of new UVs emerging from it is still there.

Right to Risk	Requirements	Based on
Right thing to do (What) - PV	To create the right experiences, we must know what to do in order to address each desired outcomes mentioned above, which is the Productive Variation (PV). Do take note that there could be easily more than one PVs for each desired outcome. This part will end only after consolidating information from UVs from below.	Root Cause Analysis, Development of Business Case, COQ measures, Brainstorming (Ideation), Interviews, Focus Group, Labs, Various problem solving tools, Data collection and analysis and Best Practices or success stories.

Risky experiences – UV *(We will be revolving around PV and its UVs until everyone is satisfied and agreed upon the risk appetite. There will also be new tolerance values to be used as key indicators for control of processes)*	These are the Unproductive Variation (UV) that will emerge if the PV above is implemented. Do take note that each PV can have more than one UV to be addressed. This is where we can identify the risk appetite of the organization when implementing a particular solution. The identification of the tolerance indicators also happens here.	Root Cause Analysis, Brainstorming, Interviews, Focus Group, Risk Assessments and mitigation plans, Safety, Health and Environment issues, Data collection and analysis, Safe Space, testing and prototypes.

While we are doing all of the above, we should also have some backings of similar approaches and success stories that relates to the problem at hand. Having done that, we now should look into addressing 'HOW' to achieve all the agreed 'WHAT to DO' (PVs) above. The next letter here is **S** that represents Success Stories to Standardization. At this point the new 'HOWs' can be created from scratch because it never existed before or embed the new way of doing thing within existing procedures or work instructions. The identified quality check point indicators and risk related tolerance indicators should also be embedded within the procedures with proper monitoring mechanisms.

Success and Standardization	Requirements	Based on
Successful Best Practices	In order to get a solution one must look beyond the organization. One way to understand this would be by knowing what are the current successful/best practices out there (beyond your cubicle, departments, company, district, states, country and so on)on a particular matter from various industries.	Internet search, Partnerships, Peer Optimization, Collaborations with interested parties and other communities of interest, Journals of Best Practices, Industry visits and Benchmarking.
Standardization (How)	We often quickly standardize(policies, procedures, work instruction, etc.) in order to reduce variations in processes; however this will certainly lead to failure even quicker if the UVs are not eliminated or put under control. Do take note that each PV above may have more than one procedure, work instruction and objectives.	Measure of activities, organization's template, processes and system objectives, understand the exact experiences to be created (PVs) through Inventions, Improvements or Innovations. Audit the experiences (positive or negative) to ensure sustainability. Issues related to safety, health and environment must be considered. Include the right quality check points to detect any form of deviation from the desired outcomes.

Well, when you have a solution in hand, we should also know whether it's working the way we wanted. So, the next letter **K** represents Key Measures and Kick Factors. Here, starting from the desired outcomes, we should be able to lay out all the measures that will allow us to know that the desired outcomes are realized successfully. These key measures are also included in the Standardization part to control all the processes involved so that they don't deviate of the initial intentions. However, the Kick Factor measures are very important for the robustness of the solution provided and sustainability. Every time we mention sustainability, it doesn't mean a solution must be static but having understood regarding the new UVs that emerged and other positive outcomes (that wasn't expected earlier, this allows the solutions to be more dynamic in nature. So, *embracing change will always be part of the solutions.*

Key measures and Kick Factors	Requirements	Based on
Key Indicators and Measures	Whatever that we are doing, we must keep tap of our inputs, process, outputs and outcomes at all times. The measurable indicators will provide us with the relevant information and knowledge to maintain our course towards the desired the desired outcome(s).	Desired outcome(s) measuring indicators, Daily operational data and reports, surveys, internal and external feedbacks, measuring and monitoring equipment.

Kick Factors for Sustainability	These are further delighting (positive) outcome(s) and also the possible undesired (negative) outcome(s) that were not captured/ not known during the risks assessment stages (lessons learned – new UVs emerge). Going back to the drawing board to resolve the new UVs is very important for sustainability and dynamism to embrace change at all times.	Desired outcome(s) measuring indicators, Daily operational data and reports, surveys, internal and external feedbacks, management audits on experiences created (positive or negative), measuring and monitoring equipment.

The DRSK framework can be an important part when addressing any kind of problem individually or in a team. When teams like Innovative and Creative Circles (ICCs) or the Kaizen problem solving teams start working on their problems, the DRSK framework will be very useful in making sure that the teams head towards a robust solution. This easy to use mechanism will ensure that every member of the team think from every angle and move forward by increasing the strength of the solutions every step of the way. Generating ideas is part of any problem solving process; however some good ideas are not developed beyond certain point because they are unable to build strength on the feasibility of implementing those ideas. So, this framework gives an opportunity to test out the ideas in a more structured manner and only park the ideas aside if it's totally not feasible.

This framework will ensure that we never address a problem in isolation, total participation from interested parties are very much encouraged through the framework. Sometimes problem solving teams just get excited with their solutions and not realizing the users of the solutions on a day to day basis will be people beyond the team. In order to make sure that the solutions are accepted, getting the end users of the solutions to participate in the problem solving process is a must. Through the DRSK framework we are able to build quality into the solutions right from the beginning stage till the right experiences that touches the belief system of an individual or group is realized. This is the clear transformation from phase Q1 to Q3 as discussed in first part.

"The Key to survival in this very fast changing world, is by understanding the holistic Dynamism of Quality in all aspects that touches our life, failing which, it will lead us directly to extinction"

ABOUT THE AUTHOR

Dr. Suresh, the managing director cum principal consultant of Strasys Solutions Sdn Bhd (Malaysia). A strong believer who advocates the importance of quality (of life),creativity, and innovation, Dr. Suresh, who is a certified quality management system (QMS) lead auditor and a PRINCE2 practitioner, brings along with him a wealth of regional knowledge and experience to share. With his more than fifteen years of experience in QMS, data management and statistical analysis, and creative and innovative thinking, coupled with both academic and industrial exposure, Dr. Suresh has authored and co-authored more than twenty knowledge-based papers, which are published as proceeding papers and journal papers.